1040EZ

INSTRUCTIONS
2015

 makes doing your taxes faster and easier.

 is the fast, safe, and free way to prepare and *e-file* your taxes.
See *www.irs.gov/freefile*.

Get a faster refund, reduce errors, and save paper. For more information on **IRS** *e-file* and Free File, see Options for *e-filing* your returns in these instructions or click on **IRS** *e-file* at IRS.gov.

2015 TAX CHANGES

See *What's New* in these instructions.

FUTURE DEVELOPMENTS

For the latest information about developments related to Form 1040EZ and its instructions, such as legislation enacted after they were published, go to *www.irs.gov/form1040ez*.

IRS

Department of the Treasury **Internal Revenue Service** IRS.gov

Jan 05, 2016   Cat. No. 12063Z

Table of Contents

Department of the Treasury

Internal Revenue Service

Introduction

About These Instructions

We have designed the instructions to make it as simple and clear as possible to file your tax return. We did this by arranging the instructions for Form 1040EZ preparation in the most helpful order.

- "Section 2—Filing Requirements" helps you decide if you even have to file.
- "Section 3—Line Instructions for Form 1040EZ" follows the main sections of the form, starting with "Top of the Form" and ending with "Signing Your Return." Cut-outs from the form connect the instructions visually to the form.
- "Section 4—After You Have Finished" gives you a checklist for completing a return. It also gives you information about filing the return.
- "Section 6—How To Get Tax Help" has topics such as how to get tax help, forms, instructions, and publications. It also gives you other useful information, such as how to check the status of a refund.

Helpful Hints

Future Developments. For the latest information about developments related to Form 1040EZ and its instructions, such as legislation enacted after they were published, go to *www.irs.gov/form1040ez*.

Filing status. We want you to use the proper filing status as you go through the instructions and tables. You can use Form 1040EZ to file as "Single" or "Married filing jointly."

If you qualify for another filing status, such as "Head of household" or "Qualifying widow(er) with dependent child," you may be able to lower your taxes by using Form 1040A or 1040 instead. See Pub. 501, Exemptions, Standard Deduction, and Filing Information, for more information.

Icons. We use icons throughout the booklet to draw your attention to special information. Here are some key icons:

 **IRS e-file.** This alerts you to many online benefits, particularly electronic tax filing, available to you at IRS.gov.

 Tip. This lets you know about possible tax benefits, helpful actions to take, or sources for additional information.

 Caution. This tells you about special rules, possible consequences to actions, and areas where you need to take special care to make correct entries.

Writing in information. Sometimes we will ask you to make an entry "in the space to the left of line . . ." The following example (using line 1) will help you make the proper entry:

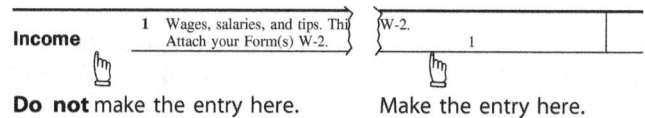

Do not make the entry here.   Make the entry here.

Section 1—Before You Begin

Even if you can use Form 1040EZ, it may benefit you to use Form 1040A or 1040 instead. See *Should You Use Another Form* in Section 2, later.

What's New

Information reporting about health coverage. If you or someone in your family had health coverage in 2015, the provider of that coverage is required to send you a Form 1095-A, 1095-B, or 1095-C (with Part III completed), that lists individuals in your family who were enrolled in the coverage and shows their months of coverage. You may use this information to help complete line 11. However, you do not need to wait to receive these forms to file your return. You may have had health care coverage for some or all of 2015 even if you didn't receive a form with this information, and you may rely on other information about your coverage to complete line 11.

For more information on why your health provider might be asking for your social security number, go to *www.irs.gov/ACASSN* .

Information reporting about employer offer of coverage. If you or someone in your family was an employee in 2015, the employer may be required to send you a Form 1095-C. Part II of Form 1095-C shows whether your employer offered you health insurance coverage and, if so, information about the offer. This information may be relevant if you purchased health insurance coverage for 2015 through the Health Insurance Marketplace and wish to claim the premium tax credit. You must file Form 1040A or 1040 to claim the premium tax credit. However, you do not need to wait to receive this form to file your return. You may rely on other information received from your employer. If you do not wish to claim the premium tax credit for 2015, you do not need the information in Part II. For more information on who is eligible for the premium tax credit, see the instructions for Form 8962.

Health care individual responsibility payment increased. If you or someone in your household didn't have qualifying health care coverage or qualify for a coverage exemption for one or more months of 2015, the amount of your shared responsibility payment may be much more this year than it was last year. Like last year, you must either:

- Indicate on line 11 that you, your spouse (if filing jointly), and anyone you can or do claim as a dependent had qualifying health care coverage throughout 2015,

- Attach Form 8965 to claim an exemption from the requirement to have health care coverage, or
- Make a shared responsibility payment if, for any month in 2015, you, your spouse (if filing jointly), or anyone you can or do claim as a dependent didn't have coverage and do not qualify for a coverage exemption.

For more information, see the instructions for line 11 and Form 8965.

Earned income credit (EIC). You may be able to take the EIC if you earned less than $14,820 ($20,330 if married filing jointly). See *Lines 8a and 8b, Earned Income Credit (EIC)* in Section 3, later.

Achieving a Better Life Experience (ABLE) account. This is a new type of savings account for individuals with disabilities and their families. For 2015, you can contribute up to $14,000. Distributions are tax-free if used to pay the beneficiary's qualified disability expenses. Don't deduct your contributions on your tax return. For details, see Pub. 907.

Due date of return. File Form 1040EZ by **April 18, 2016.** The due date is April 18, instead of April 15, because of the Emancipation Day holiday in the District of Columbia—even if you do not live in the District of Columbia. If you live in Maine or Massachusetts, you have until April 19, 2016. That is because of the Patriots' Day holiday in those states.

Public safety officers. Certain amounts received because of the death of a public safety officer are nontaxable. See Pub. 525 for details.

Certain charitable contributions. A special rule applies to cash contributions made between January 1, 2015, and April 15, 2015, to benefit the families of slain New York detectives Wenjian Liu or Rafael Ramos. See Pub. 526 for details.

Direct deposits of a refund to a *myRA®* account. You now can have your refund directly deposited to a new retirement savings program called *my*RA®. This is a starter retirement account offered by the Department of the Treasury. For more information and to open a *my*RA account online, visit *www.myRA.gov*.

Form W-2 Verification Code. The IRS is testing the use of a 16-character code to verify certain Forms W-2. If you are *e-filing* and your Form W-2 includes a code in a box labeled "Verification Code," enter the code when prompted by your software; disregard the prompt if your Form W-2 does not have the code. If you are filing a paper Form 1040, you don't have to use the code.

Earned income credit. If you didn't have a social security number (an SSN) by the due date of your 2015 return (including extensions), you can't claim the EIC on either your original or an amended 2015 return, even if you later get an SSN. Also, if a child didn't have an SSN by the due date of your return (including extensions), you can't count that child as a qualifying child in figuring the EIC on either your original or an amended 2015 return, even if that child later gets an SSN. See the instructions for lines 8a and 8b.

You May Benefit From Filing Form 1040A or 1040 in 2015

Due to the following tax law changes, you may benefit from filing Form 1040A or 1040, even if you normally file Form 1040EZ. See the instructions for Form 1040A or 1040, as applicable.

Requirement to reconcile advance payments of the premium tax credit. If you or a family member enrolled in health insurance through the Marketplace and advance payments of the premium tax credit were made to your insurance company to reduce your monthly premium payment, you must file Form 1040A or 1040 and attach Form 8962 to your return to reconcile (compare) the advance payments with your premium tax credit for the year, which you figure on Form 8962. The Marketplace is required to send Form 1095-A by February 1, 2016, listing the advance payments and other information you need to figure your premium tax credit. Use Form 1095-A to complete Form 8962. Attach Form 8962 to your return. Do not attach Form 1095-A to your return.

Information reporting about employer offer of coverage. If you or someone in your family was an employee in 2015, the employer may be required to send you a Form 1095-C. Part II of Form 1095-C shows whether your employer offered you health insurance coverage and, if so, information about the offer. This information may be relevant if you purchased health insurance coverage for 2015 through the Health Insurance Marketplace and wish to claim the premium tax credit. You must file Form 1040A or 1040 to claim the premium tax credit. However, you do not need to wait to receive this form to file your return. You may rely on other information received from your employer. If you do not wish to claim the premium tax credit for 2015, you do not need the information in Part II. For more information on who is eligible for the premium tax credit, see the instructions for Form 8962.

Earned income credit (EIC) if children lived with you. The maximum adjusted gross income (AGI) you can have and still claim the EIC has increased. You may be able to claim the credit if your AGI is less than the amount below that applies to you. The maximum investment income you can have and still claim the credit is $3,400.

You may be able to claim a larger EIC using Form 1040A or 1040 if:
- Three or more children lived with you and you earned less than $47,747 ($53,267 if married filing jointly),
- Two children lived with you and you earned less than $44,454 ($49,974 if married filing jointly), or
- One child lived with you and you earned less than $39,131 ($44,651 if married filing jointly).

Death of a Taxpayer

If a taxpayer died before filing a return for 2015, the taxpayer's spouse or personal representative may have to file and sign a return for that taxpayer. A personal representative can be an executor, administrator, or anyone who is in charge of the deceased taxpayer's property. If the deceased taxpayer did not have to file a return but had tax withheld, a return must be filed to get a refund. The person who files the return must enter "Deceased," the deceased taxpayer's name, and the date of death across the top of the return. If this information is not provided, it may delay the processing of the return.

You can file a joint return even if your spouse died in 2015 as long as you did not remarry in 2015. You can also file a joint return even if your spouse died in 2016 before filing a return for 2015. A joint return should show your spouse's 2015 income before death and your income for all of 2015. Enter "Filing as surviving spouse" in the area where you sign the return. If someone else is the personal representative, he or she also must sign.

The surviving spouse or personal representative should promptly notify all payers of income, including financial institutions, of the taxpayer's death. This will ensure the proper reporting of income earned by the taxpayer's estate or heirs. A deceased taxpayer's social security number should not be used for tax years after the year of death, except for estate tax return purposes.

Claiming a refund for a deceased taxpayer. If you are filing a joint return as a surviving spouse, you only need to file the tax return to claim the refund. If you are a court-appointed representative, file the return and include a copy of the certificate that shows your appointment. All other filers requesting the deceased taxpayer's refund must file the return and attach Form 1310.

For more details, see Tax Topic 356 at *www.irs.gov/taxtopics* or see Pub. 559.

Foreign Financial Assets

If you had foreign financial assets in 2015, you may have to file Form 8938 with your return. If you have to file Form 8938, you must use Form 1040. You cannot use Form 1040EZ. For more information about foreign financial assets and the requirements for filing Form 8938, see the Instructions for Form 8938.

Parent of a Kidnapped Child

If your child is presumed by law enforcement authorities to have been kidnapped by someone who is not a family member, you may be able to take the child into account in determining your eligibility for the head of household or qualifying widow(er) filing status, the dependency exemption, the child tax credit, and the earned income credit (EIC). But you have to file Form 1040A or 1040 to claim these benefits. For details, see Pub. 501 (Pub. 596 for the EIC).

Section 2—Filing Requirements

These rules apply to all U.S. citizens, regardless of where they live, and resident aliens.

 Have you tried IRS *e-file*? It's the fastest way to get your refund and it's free if you are eligible. Visit IRS.gov for details.

Do You Have To File?

Were you (or your spouse if filing a joint return) age 65 or older at the end of 2015? If you were born on January 1, 1951, you are considered to be age 65 at the end of 2015.

☐ **Yes.** Use Pub. 501 to see if you must file a return. If so, use Form 1040A or 1040.

☐ **No.** Use the Filing Requirement Charts, later in this Section 2, to see if you must file a return. See the *Tip* next if you have earned income.

 Even if you do not have to file a return, you should file one to get a refund of any federal income tax withheld. You also should file if you are eligible for the earned income credit.

Death of taxpayer in 2015. If you are preparing a return for someone who died in 2015, use the Filing Requirement Charts, later in this section, only if the person died at least 2 days before his or her 65th birthday. Otherwise, use Pub. 501 to see if you must file a return.

Exception for certain children under age 19 or full-time students. If certain conditions apply, you can elect to include on your return the income of a child who was under age 19 at the end of 2015 or was a full-time student under age 24 at the end of 2015. To do so, use Forms 1040 and 8814. If you make this election, your child doesn't have to file a return. For details, see Tax Topic 553 at *www.irs.gov/taxtopics* or see Form 8814.

A child born on January 1, 1992, is considered to be age 24 at the end of 2015. Do not use Form 8814 for such a child.

Resident aliens. These rules also apply if you were a resident alien. Also, you may qualify for certain tax treaty benefits. See Pub. 519 for details.

Nonresident aliens and dual-status aliens. These rules also apply if you were a nonresident alien or a dual-status alien and both of the following apply.
- You were married to a U.S. citizen or resident alien at the end of 2015.
- You elected to be taxed as a resident alien.

See Pub. 519 for details.

 Specific rules apply to determine if you are a resident alien, nonresident alien, or dual-status alien. Most nonresident aliens and dual-status aliens have different filing requirements and may have to file Form 1040NR or 1040NR-EZ. Pub. 519 discusses these requirements and other information to help aliens comply with U.S. tax law.

When Should You File?

File Form 1040EZ by **April 18, 2016** (The due date is April 18, instead of April 15, because of the Emancipation Day holiday in the District of Columbia – even if you do not live in the District of Columbia. If you live in Maine or Massachusetts, you have until April 19, 2016, because of the Patriots' Day holiday in those states.). If you file after this date, you may have to pay interest and penalties. See *What if You Cannot File on Time?* in Section 4, later, for information on how to get more time to file. There is also information about interest and penalties.

If you were serving in, or in support of, the U.S. Armed Forces in a designated combat zone or contingency operation, you may be able to file later. See Pub. 3 for details.

Instructions for Form 1040EZ

If you *e-file* your return, there is no need to mail it. See the *e-file* page earlier or IRS.gov for more information. However, if you choose to mail it, filing instructions and addresses are at the end of these instructions.

Checklist for Using Form 1040EZ

You can use Form 1040EZ if **all** the items in the following checklist apply.

☐ Your filing status is single or married filing jointly. If you were a nonresident alien at any time in 2015, see *Nonresident aliens* below.

☐ You do not claim any dependents.

☐ You do not claim any adjustments to income. See the Tax Topics for *Adjustments to Income* at *www.irs.gov/taxtopics*.

☐ If you claim a tax credit, you claim only the earned income credit. See the Tax Topics for *Tax Credits* at *www.irs.gov/taxtopics*.

☐ You (and your spouse if filing a joint return) were under age 65 and not blind at the end of 2015. If you were born on January 1, 1951, you are considered to be age 65 at the end of 2015 and cannot use Form 1040EZ.

☐ Your taxable income (line 6 of Form 1040EZ) is less than $100,000.

☐ You had only wages, salaries, tips, taxable scholarship or fellowship grants, unemployment compensation, or Alaska Permanent Fund dividends, and your taxable interest was not over $1,500.

☐ If you earned tips, they are included in boxes 5 and 7 of your Form W-2.

☐ You do not owe any household employment taxes on wages you paid to a household employee. To find out who owes these taxes, use Tax Topic 756.

☐ You are not a debtor in a chapter 11 bankruptcy case filed after October 16, 2005.

☐ Advance payments of the premium tax credit were not made for you, your spouse, or any individual you enrolled in coverage for whom no one else is claiming the personal exemption.

If you do not meet all of the requirements, you must use Form 1040A or 1040. See Tax Topic 352 at *www.irs.gov/taxtopics* to find out which form to use.

Nonresident aliens. If you were a nonresident alien at any time in 2015, your filing status must be married filing jointly to use Form 1040EZ. If your filing status isn't married filing jointly, you may have to use Form 1040NR or 1040NR-EZ. Specific rules apply to determine if you were a nonresident or resident alien. See Pub. 519 for details, including the rules for students and scholars who are aliens.

Should You Use Another Form?

Even if you can use Form 1040EZ, it may benefit you to use Form 1040A or 1040 instead. For example, you can claim the head of household filing status (which usually results in a lower tax than single) only on Form 1040A or 1040. You can claim the retirement savings contributions credit (saver's credit) only on Form 1040A or 1040. For more information on the retirement savings contributions credit, see Tax Topic 610 at *www.irs.gov/taxtopics*.

Premium tax credit. If you or your spouse, with whom you are filing a joint return, enrolled in health insurance through the Marketplace you may be eligible for a premium tax credit. You must file Form 1040A or 1040 to claim the premium tax credit. You may also be eligible to claim the premium tax credit for any dependent you claim on Form 1040A or 1040 who enrolled in health insurance through the Health Insurance Marketplace. For more information on the premium tax credit, see Pub. 974.

Tax benefits for education. If you paid higher education expenses, you may be eligible for a tax credit or deduction. You may be eligible to claim a credit (and receive a refund) even if you owe no income tax. You must file Form 1040A or 1040 to claim these tax benefits. For more information on tax benefits for education, see Pub. 970.

Itemized deductions. You can itemize deductions only on Form 1040. You will benefit by itemizing if your itemized deductions total more than your standard deduction. For 2015, the standard deduction is $6,300 for most single people and $12,600 for most married people filing a joint return. See Tax Topic 501 at *www.irs.gov/taxtopics*. But if someone can claim you (or your spouse if married) as a dependent, your standard deduction is the amount on line E of the Worksheet for Line 5 on the back of Form 1040EZ.

What Filing Status Can You Use?

Single. Use this filing status if any of the following was true on December 31, 2015.
- You were never married.
- You were legally separated, according to your state law, under a decree of divorce or separate maintenance. But if your divorce was not final (an interlocutory decree), you are considered married and cannot use the single filing status.
- You were widowed before January 1, 2015, and did not remarry in 2015.

Married filing jointly. Use this filing status if any of the following apply.
- You were married at the end of 2015, even if you did not live with your spouse at the end of 2015.
- Your spouse died in 2015, and you did not remarry in 2015.
- You were married at the end of 2015, and your spouse died in 2016 before filing a 2015 return.

If you and your spouse file jointly, report your combined income and deduct your combined allowable expenses on one return. You can file a joint return even if only one of you had income or if you did not live together all year. However, both of you must sign the return. Once you file a joint return, you cannot choose to file separate returns for that year after the due date of the return.

For information about marital status, see Pub. 501.

Joint and several tax liability. If you file a joint return, both you and your spouse are generally responsible for the tax and interest or penalties due on the return. This means that if one spouse doesn't pay the tax due, the other may have to. Or, if one spouse doesn't report the correct tax, both spouses may be responsible for any additional taxes assessed by the IRS. You may want to file separately if:
- You believe your spouse isn't reporting all of his or her income, or

- You do not want to be responsible for any taxes due if your spouse doesn't have enough tax withheld or doesn't pay enough estimated tax.

If you want to file separately, you must use Form 1040A or 1040. You cannot use Form 1040EZ. See *Innocent spouse relief* in Section 5, later.

Filing Requirement Charts

 Chart A and B users—if you have to file a return, you may be able to file Form 1040EZ. See Checklist for Using Form 1040EZ, earlier.

Chart A—For Most People

IF your filing status is . . .	AND your gross income* was at least . . .	THEN . . .
Single	$10,300	File a return
Married filing jointly**	$20,600	File a return

Gross income means all income you received in the form of money, goods, property, and services that is not exempt from tax, including any income from sources outside the United States or from the sale of your main home (even if you can exclude part or all of it).

**If you did not live with your spouse at the end of 2015 (or on the date your spouse died) and your gross income was at least $4,000, you must file a return.

Chart B—For Children and Other Dependents

If your parent (or someone else) can claim you as a dependent, use this chart.

To find out if your parent (or someone else) can claim you as a dependent, see Pub. 501.

File a return if any of the following apply.

- Your **unearned income**[1] was over $1,050.
- Your **earned income**[2] was over $6,300.
- Your **gross income**[3] was more than the **larger** of—
  - $1,050, or
  - Your earned income (up to $5,950) plus $350.

[1] **Unearned income** includes taxable interest, ordinary dividends, and capital gain distributions. It also includes unemployment compensation, taxable social security benefits, pensions, annuities, and distributions of unearned income from a trust.

[2] **Earned income** includes salaries, wages, tips, professional fees, and taxable scholarship or fellowship grants.

[3] **Gross income** is the total of your unearned and earned income.

Chart C—Other Situations When You Must File

You must file a return using Form 1040A or 1040 if **any** of the following apply for 2015.
- You owe tax from the recapture of an education credit (see **Form 8863**).
- You claim a credit for excess social security or tier 1 RRTA tax withheld.
- You claim a credit for the retirement savings contributions credit (saver's credit) (see **Form 8880**).
- You claim a premium tax credit (see **Form 8962**).
- Advance payments of the premium tax credit were made for you, your spouse, or any individual you enrolled in coverage for whom no one else is claiming the personal exemption. You or whoever enrolled you should have received Form(s) 1095-A showing the amount of the advance payments.

You must file a return using Form 1040 if **any** of the following apply for 2015.
- You owe any special taxes, such as social security and Medicare tax on tips you didn't report to your employer or on wages you received from an employer who didn't withhold these taxes.
- You owe write-in taxes, including uncollected social security and Medicare or RRTA tax on tips you reported to your employer or on group-term life insurance.
- You had net earnings from self-employment of at least $400.
- You had wages of $108.28 or more from a church or qualified church-controlled organization that is exempt from employer social security and Medicare taxes.
- You owe any recapture taxes, other than from the recapture of an education credit, including repayment of the first-time homebuyer credit (see **Form 5405**).
- You owe additional tax on a qualified plan, including an individual retirement arrangement (IRA), or other tax-favored account. But if you are filing a return only because you owe this tax, you can file **Form 5329** by itself.
- You owe household employment taxes. But if you are filing a return only because you owe this tax, you can file **Schedule H (Form 1040)** by itself.
- You (or your spouse, if filing jointly) received health savings account, Archer MSA, or Medicare Advantage MSA distributions.
- You received a Form W-2 that incorrectly includes in box 1 amounts that are payments under a Medicaid waiver program, and you cannot get a corrected W-2, or you received a Form 1099-MISC that incorrectly reported these payments to the IRS.

Instructions for Form 1040EZ

Where To Report Certain Items From 2015 Forms W-2, 1097, 1098, and 1099

File electronically. You may be eligible for free tax software that will take the guesswork out of preparing your return. Free File makes available free brand-name software and free *e-file*. Visit *www.irs.gov/freefile* for details.

Part 1	Items That Can Be Reported on Form 1040EZ	If any federal income tax withheld is shown on the forms in Part 1, include the tax withheld on Form 1040EZ, line 7.
Form	**Item and Box in Which It Should Appear**	**Where To Report on Form 1040EZ**
W-2	Wages, tips, other compensation (box 1)	Line 1
	Allocated tips (box 8)	See the instructions for Form 1040EZ, line 1
1099-G	Unemployment compensation (box 1)	Line 3
1099-INT	Interest income (box 1)	See the instructions on Form 1099-INT and the instructions for Form 1040EZ, line 2
	Interest on U.S. savings bonds and Treasury obligations (box 3)	See the instructions for Form 1040EZ, line 2
	Tax-exempt interest (box 8)	See the instructions for Form 1040EZ, line 2
1099-OID	Original issue discount (box 1)	See the instructions on Form 1099-OID
	Other periodic interest (box 2)	See the instructions on Form 1099-OID
SSA-1099	Social security benefits	See the instructions for Form 1040EZ, line 6
RRB-1099	Railroad retirement benefits	See the instructions for Form 1040EZ, line 6
Part 2	**Items That May Require Filing Another Form**	
Form	**Item and Box in Which it Should Appear**	**Other Form**
W-2	Dependent care benefits (box 10)	Must file Form 1040A or 1040
	Adoption benefits (box 12, code T)	Must file Form 1040
	Employer contributions to a health savings account (box 12, code W)	Must file Form 1040 if required to file Form 8889 (see the instructions for Form 8889)
	Amount reported in box 12, code R or Z	Must file Form 1040
	Uncollected social security and Medicare or RRTA tax (box 12, Code A, B, M, or N)	Must file Form 1040
W-2G	Gambling winnings (box 1)	Must file Form 1040
1097-BTC	Bond tax credit	Must file Form 1040
1098-E	Student loan interest (box 1)	Must file Form 1040A or 1040 to deduct
1098-T	Qualified tuition and related expenses (box 1)	Must file Form 1040A or 1040 to claim, but first see the instructions on Form 1098-T
1099-C	Canceled debt (box 2)	Generally must file Form 1040 (see Pub. 4681)
1099-DIV	Dividends and distributions	Must file Form 1040A or 1040
1099-INT	Early withdrawal penalty (box 2)	Must file Form 1040 to deduct
	Interest on U.S. savings bonds and Treasury obligations (box 3)	See the instructions on Form 1099-INT
	Foreign tax paid (box 6)	Must file Form 1040 to deduct or take a credit for the tax
1099-LTC	Long-term care and accelerated death benefits	Must file Form 1040 if required to file Form 8853 (see the instructions for Form 8853)
1099-MISC	Miscellaneous income	Must file Form 1040
1099-OID	Early withdrawal penalty (box 3)	Must file Form 1040 to deduct
1099-Q	Qualified education program payments	Must file Form 1040
1099-QA	Distributions from ABLE accounts	See the instructions for line 21 of Form 1040, Form 5329, and Pub 907
1099-R	Distributions from pensions, annuities, IRAs, etc.	Must file Form 1040A or 1040
1099-SA	Distributions from HSAs and MSAs*	Must file Form 1040

This includes distributions from Archer and Medicare Advantage MSAs.

Section 3—Line Instructions for Form 1040EZ

You may be eligible for free tax software that will take the guesswork out of preparing your return. Free File makes available free brand-name software and free *e-file*. Visit *www.irs.gov/freefile* for details.

Top of the Form

Your first name and initial	Last name	Your social security number
If a joint return, spouse's first name and initial	Last name	Spouse's social security number
Home address (number and street). If you have a P.O. box, see instructions.		Apt. no.	▲ Make sure the SSN(s) above are correct.
City, town or post office, state, and ZIP code. If you have a foreign address, also complete spaces below (see instructions).		**Presidential Election Campaign** Check here if you, or your spouse if filing jointly, want $3 to go to this fund. Checking a box below will not change your tax or refund. ☐ You
Foreign country name	Foreign province/state/county	Foreign postal code

A Name and Address

Print or type the information in the spaces provided.

If you filed a joint return for 2014 and you are filing a joint return for 2015 with the same spouse, be sure to enter your names and SSNs in the same order as on your 2014 return.

Name change. If you changed your name because of marriage, divorce, or for any other reason, be sure to report the change to the Social Security Administration (SSA) before filing your return. This prevents delays in processing your return and issuing refunds. It also safeguards your future social security benefits.

Address change. If you plan to move after filing your return, use Form 8822 to notify the IRS of your new address.

P.O. box. Enter your P.O. box number only if your post office doesn't deliver mail to your home.

Foreign address. If you have a foreign address, enter the city name on the appropriate line (do not enter any other information on that line), then also complete the spaces below that line. Do not abbreviate the country name. Follow the country's practice for entering the postal code and the name of the province, county, or state.

B Social Security Number (SSN)

An incorrect or missing SSN can increase your tax, reduce your refund, or delay your refund. To apply for an SSN, fill in Form SS-5 and return it, along with the appropriate evidence documents, to the Social Security Administration (SSA). You can get Form SS-5 online at *www.socialsecurity.gov*, from your local SSA office, or by calling the SSA at 1-800-772-1213. It usually

takes about 2 weeks to get an SSN once the SSA has all the evidence and information it needs.

Check that both the name and SSN on your Forms 1040EZ, W-2, and 1099 agree with your social security card. If they do not, your exemption(s) and any earned income credit may be disallowed, your refund may be delayed, and you may not receive credit for your social security earnings. If your Form W-2 shows an incorrect name or SSN, notify your employer or the form-issuing agent as soon as possible to make sure your earnings are credited to your social security record. If the name or SSN on your social security card is incorrect, call the SSA.

IRS individual taxpayer identification numbers (ITINs) for aliens. If you are a nonresident or resident alien and you do not have and aren't eligible to get an SSN, you must apply for an ITIN. For more information, see Form W-7 and its instructions. It takes about 7 weeks to get an ITIN.

If you already have an ITIN, enter it wherever your SSN is requested on your tax return.

An ITIN is for tax use only. It doesn't entitle you to social security benefits or change your employment or immigration status under U.S. law.

If you receive an SSN after previously using an ITIN, stop using your ITIN. Use your SSN instead. Visit a local IRS office or write a letter to the IRS explaining that you now have an SSN and want all your tax records combined under your SSN. Details about what to include with the letter and where to mail it are at *www.irs.gov/Individuals/Additional-ITIN-Information*.

Nonresident alien spouse. If your spouse is a nonresident alien, you cannot use Form 1040EZ unless he or she has either an SSN or an ITIN.

Income

Attach Form(s) W-2 here.

Enclose, but do not attach, any payment.

1	Wages, salaries, and tips. This should be shown in box 1 of your Form(s) W-2. Attach your Form(s) W-2.	1
2	Taxable interest. If the total is over $1,500, you cannot use Form 1040EZ.	2
3	Unemployment compensation and Alaska Permanent Fund dividends (see instructions).	3
4	Add lines 1, 2, and 3. This is your **adjusted gross income.**	4
5	If someone can claim you (or your spouse if a joint return) as a dependent, check the applicable box(es) below and enter the amount from the worksheet on back. ☐ **You** ☐ **Spouse** If no one can claim you (or your spouse if a joint return), enter $10,300 if **single**; $20,600 if **married filing jointly.** See back for explanation.	5
6	Subtract line 5 from line 4. If line 5 is larger than line 4, enter -0-. This is your **taxable income.**	▶ 6

(C) Presidential Election Campaign Fund

This fund helps pay for Presidential election campaigns. The fund reduces candidates' dependence on large contributions from individuals and groups and places candidates on an equal financial footing in the general election. The fund also helps pay for pediatric medical research. If you want $3 to go to this fund, check the box. If you are filing a joint return, your spouse also can have $3 go to the fund. If you check a box, your tax or refund won't change.

Income (Lines 1–6)

Rounding Off to Whole Dollars

You can round off cents to whole dollars on your return. If you do round to whole dollars, you must round all amounts. To round, drop amounts under 50 cents and increase amounts from 50 to 99 cents to the next dollar. For example, $1.39 becomes $1 and $2.50 becomes $3.

If you have to add two or more amounts to figure the amount to enter on a line, include cents when adding the amounts and round off only the total.

Example. You received two Forms W-2, one showing wages of $5,009.55 and one showing wages of $8,760.73. On Form 1040EZ, line 1, you would enter $13,770 ($5,009.55 + $8,760.73 = $13,770.28).

Refunds of State or Local Income Taxes

If you received a refund, credit, or offset of state or local income taxes in 2015, you may receive a Form 1099-G.

For the year the tax was paid to the state or other taxing authority, did you file Form 1040EZ or 1040A?

☐ **Yes.** None of your refund is taxable.

☐ **No.** You may have to report part or all of the refund as income on Form 1040 for 2015. For more information, see the Instructions for Form 1040 or Pub. 525.

Social Security Benefits

If you received social security or equivalent railroad retirement benefits, you should receive a Form SSA-1099 or Form RRB-1099. These forms will show the total benefits paid to you in 2015 and the amount of any benefits you repaid in 2015. Use the Worksheet To See if Any of Your Social Security Benefits Are Taxable, later in this Section 3. If any of your benefits are taxable, you must use Form 1040A or 1040. For more details, see Pub. 915.

Nevada, Washington, and California domestic partners

A registered domestic partner in Nevada, Washington, or California generally must report half the combined community income of the individual and his or her domestic partner. See Form 8958 and Pub. 555. If you file Form 8958, you must use Form 1040.

---

(1) Line 1, Wages, Salaries, and Tips

Enter the total of your wages, salaries, and tips. If you are filing a joint return, also include your spouse's wages, salaries, and tips. For most people, the amount to enter on this line should be shown on their Form(s) W-2 in box 1. But you must include all of your wages, salaries, and tips in the total on line 1, even if they aren't shown on your Form(s) W-2. For example, the following types of income must be included in the total on line 1.

- Wages received as a household employee for which you didn't receive a Form W-2 because your employer paid you less than $1,900 in 2015. Also, enter "HSH" and the amount not reported on a Form W-2 in the space to the left of line 1.

- Tip income you didn't report to your employer. But you must use Form 1040 and Form 4137 if (a) you received tips of $20 or more in any month and did not report the full amount to your employer, or (b) your Form(s) W-2 shows allocated tips that you must report as income. You must report the allocated tips shown on your Form(s) W-2 unless you can prove that you received less. Allocated tips should be shown on your Form(s) W-2 in box 8. They aren't included as income in box 1. See Pub. 531 for more details.

- Scholarship and fellowship grants not reported on a Form W-2. Also, enter "SCH" and the amount in the space to the

Worksheet To See if Any of Your Social Security Benefits Are Taxable

Keep for Your Records

Before you begin: ✓ If you are filing a joint return, be sure to include any amounts your spouse received when entering amounts on lines 1, 3, and 4 below.

1. Enter the amount from **box 5** of **all** your **Forms SSA-1099** and **Forms RRB-1099** . . . . **1.** _____

2. Is the amount on line 1 more than zero?

   ☐ **No.** (STOP) None of your social security benefits are taxable.

   ☐ **Yes.** Multiply line 1 by 50% (0.50) . . . . **2.** _____

3. Enter your total wages, salaries, tips, etc., from Form(s) W-2. Also, include any taxable unemployment compensation and Alaska Permanent Fund dividends you received (see the instructions for Form 1040EZ, line 3, later) . . . . **3.** _____

4. Enter your total interest income, including any tax-exempt interest . . . . **4.** _____

5. Add lines 2, 3, and 4 . . . . **5.** _____

6. If you are:
   - Single, enter $25,000
   - Married filing jointly, enter $32,000   } . . . . **6.** _____

7. Is the amount on line 6 less than the amount on line 5?

   ☐ **No.** None of your social security or railroad retirement benefits are taxable this year. You can use Form 1040EZ. **Do not** list your benefits as income.

   ☐ **Yes.** (STOP) Some of your benefits are taxable this year. You **must** use Form 1040A or 1040.

---

left of line 1. However, if you were a degree candidate, include on line 1 only the amounts you used for expenses other than tuition and course-related expenses. For example, amounts used for room, board, and travel must be reported on line 1. For more information on taxable scholarships and grants, see Pub. 970.

 You must use Form 1040A or 1040 if you received dependent care benefits for 2015. You must use Form 1040 if you received employer-provided adoption benefits for 2015.

Missing or incorrect Form W-2? Your employer is required to provide or send Form W-2 to you no later than February 1, 2016. If you do not receive it by early February, see Tax Topic 154 at *www.irs.gov/taxtopics* to find out what to do. Even if you do not get a Form W-2, you still must report your earnings on line 1. If you lose your Form W-2 or it is incorrect, ask your employer for a new one.

---

 (2) **Line 2, Taxable Interest**

If you received interest payments, you should receive a Form 1099-INT or Form 1099-OID from each payer. Report all of your taxable interest income on line 2 even if you did not receive a Form 1099-INT or 1099-OID. If you are filing a joint return, also include any taxable interest received by your spouse.

Include interest received on amounts deposited with banks, savings and loan associations, credit unions, or similar organizations. If interest was credited in 2015 on deposits that you couldn't withdraw because of the bankruptcy or insolvency of the financial institution, you may be able to exclude part or all of that interest from your 2015 income. But you must use Form 1040A or 1040 to do so. See Pub. 550 for details.

 For more information on interest received, see Tax Topic 403 at www.irs.gov/taxtopics.

You should also include taxable interest on bonds and other securities. If you cashed U.S. series EE or I savings bonds in 2015 that were issued after 1989 and you paid certain higher education expenses during the year, you may be able to exclude from income part or all of the interest on those bonds. But you must use Form 8815 and Form 1040A or 1040 to do so.

You must use Form 1040A or 1040 if you received taxable interest of more than $1,500. You also must use Form 1040A or 1040 if any of the following apply.
- You received interest as a nominee (that is, in your name but the interest income actually belongs to someone else).
- You received interest from a seller-financed mortgage and the buyer used the property as a personal residence.
- You have accrued interest from a bond.
- You are reporting original issue discount (OID) in an amount less than the amount shown on Form 1099-OID.

Instructions for Form 1040EZ

Payments, Credits, and Tax	7	Federal income tax withheld from Form(s) W-2 and 1099	7	7
	8a	**Earned income credit (EIC)** (see instructions)	8a	8a
	b	Nontaxable combat pay election 8b		
	9	Add lines 7 and 8a. These are your **total payments and credits.** ▶	9	9
	10	**Tax.** Use the amount on **line 6 above** to find your tax in the tax table in the instructions. Then, enter the tax from the table on this line.	10	10
	11	Health care: individual responsibility (see instructions) Full-year cov □	11	11
	12	Add lines 10 and 11. This is your **total tax.**	12	12

- You are reducing your interest income on a bond by the amount of amortizable bond premium.
- You are claiming the exclusion of interest from series EE or I U.S. savings bonds issued after 1989.
- You owned or had authority over one or more foreign financial accounts (such as bank accounts) with a combined value over $10,000 at any time during 2015.

Tax-Exempt Interest

If you received tax-exempt interest, such as interest on municipal bonds, each payer should send you a Form 1099-INT. Your tax-exempt interest should be shown in box 8 of Form 1099-INT. Enter "TEI" and the amount in the space to the left of line 2. Do not include tax-exempt interest in the total on line 2.

Line 3, Unemployment Compensation and Alaska Permanent Fund Dividends

Unemployment compensation. You should receive a Form 1099-G showing in box 1 the total unemployment compensation paid to you in 2015. Report this amount on line 3. If you are filing a joint return, also report on line 3 any unemployment compensation received by your spouse. If you made contributions to a governmental unemployment compensation program or a governmental paid family leave program, reduce the amount you report on line 3 by those contributions.

If you received an overpayment of unemployment compensation in 2015 and you repaid any of it in 2015, subtract the amount you repaid from the total amount you received. Enter the result on line 3. However, if the result is zero or less, enter -0- on line 3. Also, enter "Repaid" and the amount you repaid in the space to the left of line 3. If, in 2015, you repaid unemployment compensation that you included in gross income in an earlier year, you can deduct the amount repaid; but you must use Form 1040 to do so. See Pub. 525 for details.

Alaska Permanent Fund dividends. If you received Alaska Permanent Fund dividends, include them in the total on line 3. If you are filing a joint return, also report on line 3 any Alaska Permanent Fund dividends received by your spouse. You cannot use Form 1040EZ if you (or your spouse) received any other kind of dividends.

If a child's interest and Alaska Permanent Fund dividends total more than $2,100, he or she may be required to file Form 8615 and Form 1040A or 1040 instead of Form 1040EZ. The child's parent may, however, be able to include the child's income on the parent's return. If so, the child need not file a return, but the parent must file Form 8814 and Form 1040. For more information, see *Exception for certain children under age 19 or full-time students* in Section 2, earlier, and Pub. 929.

Line 6, Taxable Income

Your taxable income and filing status will determine the amount of tax you enter on line 10.

Figuring taxable income incorrectly is one of the most common errors on Form 1040EZ. So please take extra care when subtracting line 5 from line 4.

If you received Forms SSA-1099 or RRB-1099 (showing amounts treated as social security) use the Worksheet To See if Any of Your Social Security Benefits Are Taxable, earlier in this Section 3, to determine if you can file Form 1040EZ.

Payments, Credits, and Tax (Lines 7–11)

Line 7, Federal Income Tax Withheld

Enter the total amount of federal income tax withheld. This should be shown on your 2015 Form(s) W-2 in box 2.

If you received 2015 Form(s) 1099-INT, 1099-G, or 1099-OID showing federal income tax withheld, include the tax withheld in the total on line 7. This should be shown in box 4 of these forms.

8 Lines 8a and 8b, Earned Income Credit (EIC)

What Is the EIC?

The EIC is a credit for certain people who work. The credit may give you a refund even if you do not owe any tax or did not have any tax withheld.

Note. If you have a qualifying child (defined in Step 1, later), you may be able to take the credit, but you must use Schedule EIC and Form 1040A or 1040 to do so. For details, see Pub. 596.

To Take the EIC:
- Follow Steps 1 through 3 next.
- Complete the *Earned Income Credit (EIC) Worksheet—Lines 8a and 8b*, later, or let the IRS figure the credit for you.

For help in determining if you are eligible for the EIC, go to www.irs.gov/eitc and use the "EITC Assistant." This service is available in English and Spanish.

If you take the EIC even though you aren't eligible and it is determined that your error is due to reckless or intentional disregard of the EIC rules, you won't be allowed to take the credit for 2 years even if you are otherwise eligible to do so. If you fraudulently take the EIC, you won't be allowed to take the credit for 10 years. See Form 8862, who must file *under* Definitions and Special Rules, *later. You also may have to pay penalties.*

Step 1 All Filers

1. Is the amount on Form 1040EZ, line 4, less than $14,820 ($20,330 if married filing jointly)?

    ☐ **Yes.** Go to question 2. ☐ **No.** (STOP)

    You cannot take the credit.

2. Do you, and your spouse if filing a joint return, have a social security number that allows you to work and is valid for EIC purposes (explained later in *Social security number (SSN)* under *Definitions and Special Rules*)?

    ☐ **Yes.** Go to question 3. ☐ **No.** (STOP)

    You cannot take the credit. Enter "No" in the space to the left of line 8a.

3. Did you have $3,400 or less of taxable and tax-exempt interest?

    ☐ **Yes.** Go to question 4. ☐ **No.** (STOP)

    You cannot take the credit.

4. Were you, or your spouse if filing a joint return, at least age 25 but under age 65 at the end of 2015? (Check "Yes" if you, or your spouse if filing a joint return, were born after December 31, 1950, and before January 2, 1991). If your spouse died in 2015 (or if you are preparing a return for someone who died in 2015), see Pub. 596 before you answer.

    ☐ **Yes.** Go to question 5. ☐ **No.** (STOP)

    You cannot take the credit.

5. Was your main home, and your spouse's if filing a joint return, in the United States for more than half of 2015? Members of the military stationed outside the United States, see *Members of the military* under *Definitions and Special Rules*, later, before you answer.

    ☐ **Yes.** Go to question 6. ☐ **No.** (STOP)

    You cannot take the credit. Enter "No" in the space to the left of line 8a.

6. Are you filing a joint return for 2015?

    ☐ **Yes.** Skip questions 7 and 8; go to Step 2. ☐ **No.** Go to question 7.

7. Look at the qualifying child conditions next. Could you be a qualifying child of another person in 2015? (Check "No" if the other person isn't required to file, and isn't filing, a 2015 return or is filing a 2015 return only as a claim for refund (defined under *Definitions and Special Rules*, later.))

    ☐ **Yes.** (STOP) ☐ **No.** Go to question 8.

    You cannot take the credit. Enter "No" in the space to the left of line 8a.

A **qualifying child** for the EIC is a child who is your...

Son, daughter, stepchild, foster child, brother, sister, stepbrother, stepsister, half brother, half sister, or a descendant of any of them (for example, your grandchild, niece, or nephew).

was...

Under age 19 at the end of 2015 and younger than you (or your spouse if filing jointly)

or

Under age 24 at the end of 2015, a student (defined later), and younger than you (or your spouse if filing jointly)

or

Any age and permanently and totally disabled (defined later)

Who isn't filing a joint return for 2015 or is filing a joint return for 2015 only as a claim for refund (defined later)

Who lived with you in the United States for more than half of 2015.

 You can't take the credit for a child who didn't live with you for more than half the year, even if you paid most of the child's living expenses. The IRS may ask you for documents to show you lived with each qualifying child. Documents you might want to keep for this purpose include school and child care records and other records that show your child's address.

 If the child didn't live with you for more than half of 2015 because of a temporary absence, birth, death, or kidnapping, see Exception to time lived with you, under Definitions and Special Rules, later.

 Special rules apply if the child was married or also meets the conditions to be a qualifying child of another person (other than your spouse if filing a joint return). For details, see Tax Topic 601 at www.irs.gov/taxtopics or see Pub. 596.

8. Can you be claimed as a dependent on someone else's 2015 tax return?

☐ **Yes.** (STOP)

You cannot take the credit.

☐ **No.** Go to Step 2.

Step 2

1. Complete the following worksheet to figure your earned income:

Earned Income Worksheet

1. Enter the amount from Form 1040EZ, line 1 . . . . _____

2. Enter any amount included on Form 1040EZ, line 1, that is a taxable scholarship or fellowship grant not reported on Form W-2 . . . . _____

3. Enter any amount included on Form 1040EZ, line 1, that you received for work performed while an inmate in a penal institution. (Enter "PRI" and the same amount on the dotted line next to Form 1040EZ, line 1) . . . . _____

4. Enter any amount included on Form 1040EZ, line 1, that you received as a pension or annuity from a nonqualified deferred compensation plan or a nongovernmental section 457 plan. (Enter "DFC" and the same amount on the dotted line next to Form 1040EZ, line 1). This amount may be shown in box 11 of Form W-2. If you received such an amount but box 11 is blank, contact your employer for the amount received . . . . _____

5. Add lines 2, 3, and 4 . . . . _____

6. Subtract line 5 from line 1 . . . . _____

7. Enter all your nontaxable combat pay if you elect to include it in earned income. Also enter this amount on Form 1040EZ, line 8b. See *Combat pay, nontaxable*, under *Definitions and Special Rules*, later . . . . _____

 Electing to include nontaxable combat pay may increase or decrease your EIC. Figure the credit with and without your nontaxable combat pay before making the election.

8. Add lines 6 and 7. **This is your earned income** . . . . _____

---

2. Is your earned income less than $14,820 ($20,330 if married filing jointly)?

☐ **Yes.** Go to Step 3.

☐ **No.** (STOP)

You cannot take the credit.

Earned Income Credit (EIC) Worksheet—Lines 8a and 8b

Keep for Your Records

1. Enter your earned income from Step 2, earlier .... 1. _____

2. Look up the amount on line 1 above in the EIC Table, later, to find the credit. Be sure you use the correct column for your filing status (single or married filing jointly).

   Enter the credit here .... 2. _____

   (STOP) If line 2 is zero, You cannot take the credit. Enter "No" in the space to the left of line 8a.

3. Enter the amount from Form 1040EZ, line 4 .... 3. _____

4. Are the amounts on lines 3 and 1 the same?

   ☐ **Yes.** Skip line 5; enter the amount from line 2 on line 6.

   ☐ **No.** Go to line 5.

5. Is the amount on line 3 less than $8,250 ($13,750 if married filing jointly)?

   ☐ **Yes.** Leave line 5 blank; enter the amount from line 2 on line 6.

   ☐ **No.** Look up the amount on line 3 in the EIC Table, later, to find the credit. Be sure you use the correct column for your filing status (single or married filing jointly).

   Enter the credit here .... 5. _____

   Look at the amounts on lines 5 and 2. Then, enter the **smaller** amount on line 6.

6. **Earned income credit.** Enter this amount on Form 1040EZ, **line 8a** .... 6. _____

⚠ **CAUTION** *If your EIC for a year after 1996 was reduced or disallowed, see* Form 8862, who must file *under Definitions and Special Rules, later, to find out if you must file Form 8862 to take the credit for 2015.*

Step 3 How To Figure the Credit

1. Do you want the IRS to figure the credit for you?

   ☐ **Yes.** See *Credit figured by the IRS* under *Definitions and Special Rules,* later.

   ☐ **No.** Go to the *Earned Income Credit (EIC) Worksheet—Lines 8a and 8b*.

Definitions and Special Rules

(listed in alphabetical order)

Claim for refund. A claim for refund is a return filed only to get a refund of withheld income tax or estimated tax paid. A return isn't a claim for refund if you claim the earned income credit or any other similar refundable credit.

Combat pay, nontaxable. If you were a member of the U.S. Armed Forces who served in a combat zone, certain pay is excluded from your income. See *Combat Zone Exclusion* in Pub. 3. You can elect to include this pay in your earned income when figuring the EIC. The amount of your nontaxable combat pay should be shown in box 12 of Form(s) W-2 with code Q. If you are filing a joint return and both you and your spouse received nontaxable combat pay, you can each make your own election. In other words, if one of you makes the election, the other one can also make it but doesn't have to.

Credit figured by the IRS. To have the IRS figure your EIC:

1. Enter "EIC" in the space to the left of line 8a on Form 1040EZ.

2. Be sure you enter the nontaxable combat pay you elect to include in earned income on Form 1040EZ, line 8b. See *Combat pay, nontaxable,* earlier.

3. If your EIC for a year after 1996 was reduced or disallowed, see *Form 8862, who must file,* later.

Exception to time lived with you. Temporary absences by you or the child for special circumstances, such as school, vacation, business, medical care, military service, or detention in a juvenile facility, count as time lived with you. A child is considered to have lived with you for more than half of 2015 if the child was born or died in 2015 and your home was this child's home for more than half the time he or she was alive in 2015. Special rules apply to members of the military (see *Members of the military,* later) or if the child was kidnapped (see Pub. 596).

Form 8862, who must file. You must file Form 8862 if your EIC for a year after 1996 was reduced or disallowed for any reason other than a math or clerical error. But do not file Form 8862 if either of the following applies.

1. You filed Form 8862 for another year, the EIC was allowed for that year, and your EIC has not been reduced or disallowed again for any reason other than a math or clerical error.

2. The only reason your EIC was reduced or disallowed in the earlier year was because it was determined that a child listed on Schedule EIC was not your qualifying child.

   Also, do not file Form 8862 or take the credit for:
   - 2 years after the most recent tax year for which there was a final determination that your EIC claim was due to reckless or intentional disregard of the EIC rules, or

- 10 years after the most recent tax year for which there was a final determination that your EIC claim was due to fraud.

Members of the military. If you were on extended active duty outside the United States, your main home is considered to be in the United States during that duty period. Extended active duty is military duty ordered for an indefinite period or for a period of more than 90 days. Once you begin serving extended active duty, you are considered to be on extended active duty even if you do not serve more than 90 days.

Permanently and totally disabled. A person is permanently and totally disabled if, at any time in 2015, the person could not engage in any substantial gainful activity because of a physical or mental condition and a doctor has determined that this condition has lasted or can be expected to last continuously for at least a year or can be expected to lead to death.

Social security number (SSN). For the EIC, a valid SSN is a number issued by the Social Security Administration unless "Not Valid for Employment" is printed on the social security card and the number was issued solely to allow the recipient of the SSN to apply for or receive a federally funded benefit. However, if "Valid for Work Only with DHS Authorization" is printed on your social security card, your SSN is valid for EIC purposes only as long as the DHS authorization is still valid.

To find out how to get an SSN, see *Social Security Number (SSN)*, earlier, at the beginning of this Section 3. If you will not have an SSN by the date your return is due, see *What if You Cannot File on Time?* in Section 4, later.

If you didn't have an SSN by the due date of your 2015 return (including extensions), you can't claim the EIC on either your original or an amended 2015 return, even if you later get an SSN. Also, if a child didn't have an SSN by the due date of your return (including extensions), you can't count that child as a qualifying child in figuring the EIC on either your original or an amended 2015 return, even if that child later gets an SSN.

Student. For purposes of this credit, a student is a child who during any part of 5 calendar months of 2015 was enrolled as a full-time student at a school, or took a full-time, on-farm training course given by a school or a state, county, or local government agency. A school includes a technical, trade, or mechanical school. It doesn't include an on-the-job training course, correspondence school, or a school offering courses only through the Internet.

Welfare benefits, effect of credit on. Any refund you receive as a result of taking the EIC cannot be counted as income when determining if you or anyone else is eligible for benefits or assistance, or how much you or anyone else can receive, under any federal program or under any state or local program financed in whole or in part with federal funds. These programs include Temporary Assistance for Needy Families (TANF), Medicaid, Supplemental Security Income (SSI), and Supplemental Nutrition Assistance Program (food stamps). In addition, when determining eligibility, the refund cannot be counted as a resource for at least 12 months after you receive it. Check with your local benefits coordinator to find out if your refund will affect your benefits.

2015 Earned Income Credit (EIC) Table

 CAUTION This is not a tax table.

Follow the two steps below to find your credit.

Step 1. Read down the "At least—But less than" columns and find the line that includes the amount you were told to look up from your EIC Worksheet, earlier.

Step 2. Then, read across the column for your filing status (Single or Married filing jointly). Enter the credit from that column on your EIC Worksheet.

At least	But less than	Single	Married filing jointly	At least	But less than	Single	Married filing jointly	At least	But less than	Single	Married filing jointly	At least	But less than	Single	Married filing jointly
$1	$50	$2	$2	3,000	3,050	231	231	6,000	6,050	461	461	9,000	9,050	443	503
50	100	6	6	3,050	3,100	235	235	6,050	6,100	465	465	9,050	9,100	439	503
100	150	10	10	3,100	3,150	239	239	6,100	6,150	469	469	9,100	9,150	436	503
150	200	13	13	3,150	3,200	243	243	6,150	6,200	472	472	9,150	9,200	432	503
200	250	17	17	3,200	3,250	247	247	6,200	6,250	476	476	9,200	9,250	428	503
250	300	21	21	3,250	3,300	251	251	6,250	6,300	480	480	9,250	9,300	424	503
300	350	25	25	3,300	3,350	254	254	6,300	6,350	484	484	9,300	9,350	420	503
350	400	29	29	3,350	3,400	258	258	6,350	6,400	488	488	9,350	9,400	417	503
400	450	33	33	3,400	3,450	262	262	6,400	6,450	492	492	9,400	9,450	413	503
450	500	36	36	3,450	3,500	266	266	6,450	6,500	495	495	9,450	9,500	409	503
500	550	40	40	3,500	3,550	270	270	6,500	6,550	499	499	9,500	9,550	405	503
550	600	44	44	3,550	3,600	273	273	6,550	6,600	503	503	9,550	9,600	401	503
600	650	48	48	3,600	3,650	277	277	6,600	6,650	503	503	9,600	9,650	397	503
650	700	52	52	3,650	3,700	281	281	6,650	6,700	503	503	9,650	9,700	394	503
700	750	55	55	3,700	3,750	285	285	6,700	6,750	503	503	9,700	9,750	390	503
750	800	59	59	3,750	3,800	289	289	6,750	6,800	503	503	9,750	9,800	386	503
800	850	63	63	3,800	3,850	293	293	6,800	6,850	503	503	9,800	9,850	382	503
850	900	67	67	3,850	3,900	296	296	6,850	6,900	503	503	9,850	9,900	378	503
900	950	71	71	3,900	3,950	300	300	6,900	6,950	503	503	9,900	9,950	374	503
950	1,000	75	75	3,950	4,000	304	304	6,950	7,000	503	503	9,950	10,000	371	503
1,000	1,050	78	78	4,000	4,050	308	308	7,000	7,050	503	503	10,000	10,050	367	503
1,050	1,100	82	82	4,050	4,100	312	312	7,050	7,100	503	503	10,050	10,100	363	503
1,100	1,150	86	86	4,100	4,150	316	316	7,100	7,150	503	503	10,100	10,150	359	503
1,150	1,200	90	90	4,150	4,200	319	319	7,150	7,200	503	503	10,150	10,200	355	503
1,200	1,250	94	94	4,200	4,250	323	323	7,200	7,250	503	503	10,200	10,250	352	503
1,250	1,300	98	98	4,250	4,300	327	327	7,250	7,300	503	503	10,250	10,300	348	503
1,300	1,350	101	101	4,300	4,350	331	331	7,300	7,350	503	503	10,300	10,350	344	503
1,350	1,400	105	105	4,350	4,400	335	335	7,350	7,400	503	503	10,350	10,400	340	503
1,400	1,450	109	109	4,400	4,450	339	339	7,400	7,450	503	503	10,400	10,450	336	503
1,450	1,500	113	113	4,450	4,500	342	342	7,450	7,500	503	503	10,450	10,500	332	503
1,500	1,550	117	117	4,500	4,550	346	346	7,500	7,550	503	503	10,500	10,550	329	503
1,550	1,600	120	120	4,550	4,600	350	350	7,550	7,600	503	503	10,550	10,600	325	503
1,600	1,650	124	124	4,600	4,650	354	354	7,600	7,650	503	503	10,600	10,650	321	503
1,650	1,700	128	128	4,650	4,700	358	358	7,650	7,700	503	503	10,650	10,700	317	503
1,700	1,750	132	132	4,700	4,750	361	361	7,700	7,750	503	503	10,700	10,750	313	503
1,750	1,800	136	136	4,750	4,800	365	365	7,750	7,800	503	503	10,750	10,800	309	503
1,800	1,850	140	140	4,800	4,850	369	369	7,800	7,850	503	503	10,800	10,850	306	503
1,850	1,900	143	143	4,850	4,900	373	373	7,850	7,900	503	503	10,850	10,900	302	503
1,900	1,950	147	147	4,900	4,950	377	377	7,900	7,950	503	503	10,900	10,950	298	503
1,950	2,000	151	151	4,950	5,000	381	381	7,950	8,000	503	503	10,950	11,000	294	503
2,000	2,050	155	155	5,000	5,050	384	384	8,000	8,050	503	503	11,000	11,050	290	503
2,050	2,100	159	159	5,050	5,100	388	388	8,050	8,100	503	503	11,050	11,100	286	503
2,100	2,150	163	163	5,100	5,150	392	392	8,100	8,150	503	503	11,100	11,150	283	503
2,150	2,200	166	166	5,150	5,200	396	396	8,150	8,200	503	503	11,150	11,200	279	503
2,200	2,250	170	170	5,200	5,250	400	400	8,200	8,250	503	503	11,200	11,250	275	503
2,250	2,300	174	174	5,250	5,300	404	404	8,250	8,300	501	503	11,250	11,300	271	503
2,300	2,350	178	178	5,300	5,350	407	407	8,300	8,350	497	503	11,300	11,350	267	503
2,350	2,400	182	182	5,350	5,400	411	411	8,350	8,400	493	503	11,350	11,400	264	503
2,400	2,450	186	186	5,400	5,450	415	415	8,400	8,450	489	503	11,400	11,450	260	503
2,450	2,500	189	189	5,450	5,500	419	419	8,450	8,500	485	503	11,450	11,500	256	503
2,500	2,550	193	193	5,500	5,550	423	423	8,500	8,550	482	503	11,500	11,550	252	503
2,550	2,600	197	197	5,550	5,600	426	426	8,550	8,600	478	503	11,550	11,600	248	503
2,600	2,650	201	201	5,600	5,650	430	430	8,600	8,650	474	503	11,600	11,650	244	503
2,650	2,700	205	205	5,650	5,700	434	434	8,650	8,700	470	503	11,650	11,700	241	503
2,700	2,750	208	208	5,700	5,750	438	438	8,700	8,750	466	503	11,700	11,750	237	503
2,750	2,800	212	212	5,750	5,800	442	442	8,750	8,800	462	503	11,750	11,800	233	503
2,800	2,850	216	216	5,800	5,850	446	446	8,800	8,850	459	503	11,800	11,850	229	503
2,850	2,900	220	220	5,850	5,900	449	449	8,850	8,900	455	503	11,850	11,900	225	503
2,900	2,950	224	224	5,900	5,950	453	453	8,900	8,950	451	503	11,900	11,950	221	503
2,950	3,000	228	228	5,950	6,000	457	457	8,950	9,000	447	503	11,950	12,000	218	503

(Continued)

Earned Income Credit (EIC) Table - Continued   (Caution. This is **not** a tax table.)

If the amount you are looking up from the worksheet is—		And your filing status is—	
At least	But less than	Single	Married filing jointly
		Your credit is—	
12,000	12,050	214	503
12,050	12,100	210	503
12,100	12,150	206	503
12,150	12,200	202	503
12,200	12,250	199	503
12,250	12,300	195	503
12,300	12,350	191	503
12,350	12,400	187	503
12,400	12,450	183	503
12,450	12,500	179	503
12,500	12,550	176	503
12,550	12,600	172	503
12,600	12,650	168	503
12,650	12,700	164	503
12,700	12,750	160	503
12,750	12,800	156	503
12,800	12,850	153	503
12,850	12,900	149	503
12,900	12,950	145	503
12,950	13,000	141	503
13,000	13,050	137	503
13,050	13,100	133	503
13,100	13,150	130	503
13,150	13,200	126	503
13,200	13,250	122	503
13,250	13,300	118	503
13,300	13,350	114	503
13,350	13,400	111	503
13,400	13,450	107	503
13,450	13,500	103	503
13,500	13,550	99	503
13,550	13,600	95	503
13,600	13,650	91	503
13,650	13,700	88	503
13,700	13,750	84	503
13,750	13,800	80	501
13,800	13,850	76	498
13,850	13,900	72	494
13,900	13,950	68	490
13,950	14,000	65	486
14,000	14,050	61	482
14,050	14,100	57	479
14,100	14,150	53	475
14,150	14,200	49	471
14,200	14,250	46	467
14,250	14,300	42	463
14,300	14,350	38	459
14,350	14,400	34	456
14,400	14,450	30	452
14,450	14,500	26	448

If the amount you are looking up from the worksheet is—		And your filing status is—	
At least	But less than	Single	Married filing jointly
		Your credit is—	
14,500	14,550	23	444
14,550	14,600	19	440
14,600	14,650	15	436
14,650	14,700	11	433
14,700	14,750	7	429
14,750	14,800	3	425
14,800	14,850	*	421
14,850	14,900	0	417
14,900	14,950	0	413
14,950	15,000	0	410
15,000	15,050	0	406
15,050	15,100	0	402
15,100	15,150	0	398
15,150	15,200	0	394
15,200	15,250	0	391
15,250	15,300	0	387
15,300	15,350	0	383
15,350	15,400	0	379
15,400	15,450	0	375
15,450	15,500	0	371
15,500	15,550	0	368
15,550	15,600	0	364
15,600	15,650	0	360
15,650	15,700	0	356
15,700	15,750	0	352
15,750	15,800	0	348
15,800	15,850	0	345
15,850	15,900	0	341
15,900	15,950	0	337
15,950	16,000	0	333
16,000	16,050	0	329
16,050	16,100	0	326
16,100	16,150	0	322
16,150	16,200	0	318
16,200	16,250	0	314
16,250	16,300	0	310
16,300	16,350	0	306
16,350	16,400	0	303
16,400	16,450	0	299
16,450	16,500	0	295
16,500	16,550	0	291
16,550	16,600	0	287
16,600	16,650	0	283
16,650	16,700	0	280
16,700	16,750	0	276
16,750	16,800	0	272
16,800	16,850	0	268
16,850	16,900	0	264
16,900	16,950	0	260
16,950	17,000	0	257

If the amount you are looking up from the worksheet is—		And your filing status is—	
At least	But less than	Single	Married filing jointly
		Your credit is—	
17,000	17,050	0	253
17,050	17,100	0	249
17,100	17,150	0	245
17,150	17,200	0	241
17,200	17,250	0	238
17,250	17,300	0	234
17,300	17,350	0	230
17,350	17,400	0	226
17,400	17,450	0	222
17,450	17,500	0	218
17,500	17,550	0	215
17,550	17,600	0	211
17,600	17,650	0	207
17,650	17,700	0	203
17,700	17,750	0	199
17,750	17,800	0	195
17,800	17,850	0	192
17,850	17,900	0	188
17,900	17,950	0	184
17,950	18,000	0	180
18,000	18,050	0	176
18,050	18,100	0	173
18,100	18,150	0	169
18,150	18,200	0	165
18,200	18,250	0	161
18,250	18,300	0	157
18,300	18,350	0	153
18,350	18,400	0	150
18,400	18,450	0	146
18,450	18,500	0	142
18,500	18,550	0	138
18,550	18,600	0	134
18,600	18,650	0	130
18,650	18,700	0	127
18,700	18,750	0	123
18,750	18,800	0	119
18,800	18,850	0	115
18,850	18,900	0	111
18,900	18,950	0	107
18,950	19,000	0	104
19,000	19,050	0	100
19,050	19,100	0	96
19,100	19,150	0	92
19,150	19,200	0	88
19,200	19,250	0	85
19,250	19,300	0	81
19,300	19,350	0	77
19,350	19,400	0	73
19,400	19,450	0	69
19,450	19,500	0	65

If the amount you are looking up from the worksheet is—		And your filing status is—	
At least	But less than	Single	Married filing jointly
		Your credit is—	
19,500	19,550	0	62
19,550	19,600	0	58
19,600	19,650	0	54
19,650	19,700	0	50
19,700	19,750	0	46
19,750	19,800	0	42
19,800	19,850	0	39
19,850	19,900	0	35
19,900	19,950	0	31
19,950	20,000	0	27
20,000	20,050	0	23
20,050	20,100	0	20
20,100	20,150	0	16
20,150	20,200	0	12
20,200	20,250	0	8
20,250	20,300	0	4
20,300	20,330	0	**

* If the amount you are looking up from the worksheet is at least $14,800 but less than $14,820, your credit is $1. If the amount you are looking up from the worksheet is $14,820 or more, you cannot take the credit.

** If the amount you are looking up from the worksheet is at least $20,300 but less than $20,330, your credit is $1. If the amount you are looking up from the worksheet is $20,330 or more, you cannot take the credit.

Instructions for Form 1040EZ

Line 9

Add lines 7 and 8a. Enter the total on line 9.

Amount paid with request for extension of time to file. If you requested an automatic extension of time to file Form 1040EZ using Form 4868, include on line 9 any amount paid with that form. Also include any amount you paid by electronic funds withdrawal, credit or debit card, or the Electronic Federal Tax Payment System (EFTPS) to get an extension. If you paid by credit or debit card, do not include on line 9 the convenience fee you were charged. To the left of line 9, enter "Form 4868" and show the amount paid.

 If you pay your taxes by credit or debit card, you may be able to deduct the related credit or debit card convenience fees on your 2016 tax return, but you must file Form 1040 to do so.

 Line 10, Tax

Do you want the IRS to figure your tax for you?

☐ **Yes.** See chapter 30 of Pub. 17 for details, including who is eligible and what to do. If you have paid too much, we will send you a refund. If you did not pay enough, we will send you a bill.

☐ **No.** Use the Tax Table later in these instructions.

Refund

If line 13a is under $1, we will send the refund only on written request.

If you want to check the status of your refund, see *Refund Information* in Section 6, later. Information about your return will generally be available within 24 hours after the IRS receives your e-filed return, or 4 weeks after you mail your paper return. If you filed Form 8379 with your return, wait 14 weeks (11 weeks if you filed electronically).

 If your refund is large, you may want to decrease the amount of income tax withheld from your pay by filing a new Form W-4. See Income tax withholding and estimated tax payments for 2016 in Section 5, later.

Effect of refund on benefits. Any refund you receive cannot be counted as income when determining if you or anyone else is eligible for benefits or assistance, or how much you or anyone else can receive, under any federal program or under any state or local program financed in whole or in part with federal funds. These programs include Temporary Assistance for Needy Families (TANF), Medicaid, Supplemental Security Income (SSI), and Supplemental Nutrition Assistance Program (food stamps). In addition, when determining eligibility, the refund cannot be counted as a resource for at least 12 months after you receive it. Check with your local benefit coordinator to find out if your refund will affect your benefits.

Refund Offset

If you owe past-due federal tax, state income tax, state unemployment compensation debts, child support, spousal support, or certain federal nontax debts, such as student loans, all or part of the refund on line 13a may be used (offset) to pay the past-due amount. Offsets for federal taxes are made by the IRS. All other offsets are made by the Treasury Department's Bureau of the Fiscal Service. For federal tax offsets, you will receive a notice from the IRS. For all other offsets, you will receive a notice from the Fiscal Service. To find out if you may have an offset or if you have a question about it, contact the agency to which you owe the debt.

Injured spouse. If you file a joint return and your spouse has not paid past-due federal tax, state income tax, state unemployment compensation debts, child support, spousal support, or a federal nontax debt, such as a student loan, part or all of the refund on line 13a may be used (offset) to pay the past-due amount. But your part of the refund may be refunded to you if certain conditions apply and you complete Form 8379. For details, see Tax Topic 203 at *www.irs.gov/taxtopics* or see Form 8379.

 Line 11, Health Care: Individual Responsibility

You must either:
- Have qualifying health care coverage for every month of 2015 for yourself, your spouse (if filing jointly), and anyone you can or do claim as a dependent, (You are treated as having coverage for any month in which you have coverage for at least 1 day of the month),
- Qualify for an exemption from the requirement to have health care coverage, or
- Make a shared responsibility payment with your tax return and enter the amount on this line.

If you had qualifying health care coverage (called minimum essential coverage) for every month of 2015 for yourself, your spouse (if filing jointly), and anyone you can or do claim as a dependent, check the box on this line and leave the entry space blank.

Otherwise, do not check the box on this line. If you, your spouse (if filing jointly) or someone you can or do claim as a dependent didn't have coverage for each month of 2015 you must either claim a coverage exemption on Form 8965 or report a shared responsibility payment on line 11. See the instructions for Form 8965 for information on coverage exemptions and figuring the shared responsibility payment.

You can check the box even if:
- A dependent child who was born or adopted during the year was not covered by your insurance during the month of or months before birth or adoption (but the child must have had minimum essential coverage every month of 2015 following the birth or adoption), or
- A spouse or dependent who died during the year was not covered by your insurance during the month of death and months after death (but he or she must have had minimum

essential coverage every month of 2015 he or she was alive).

If you can be claimed as a dependent, do not check the box on this line. Leave the entry space blank. You do not need to attach Form 8965 or see its instructions.

If you or someone in your household had minimum essential coverage in 2015, the provider of that coverage is required to send you a Form 1095-A, 1095-B, or 1095-C (with Part III completed) that lists individuals in your family who were enrolled in the coverage and shows their months of coverage.
- Individuals enrolled in health insurance coverage through the Marketplace generally receive this information on Form 1095-A, Health Insurance Marketplace Statement.
- Individuals enrolled in health insurance coverage provided by their employer generally receive this information on either Form 1095-B, Health Coverage, or on Form 1095-C, Employer-Provided Health Insurance Offer and Coverage.
- Individuals enrolled in a government-sponsored health program or in other types of coverage generally receive this information on Form 1095-B, Health Coverage.

Even if you haven't received one of these forms, you may have had health care coverage and can rely on other information you have about your coverage to complete line 11.

Your health care coverage provider may have asked for your social security number. To understand why, go to *www.irs.gov/ACASSN*.

Minimum essential coverage. Most health care coverage that people have is minimum essential coverage.

Minimum essential coverage includes:
- Most types of health care coverage provided by your employer,
- Many types of government-sponsored health care coverage including Medicare, most Medicaid coverage, and most health care coverage provided to veterans and active duty service members,
- Certain types of health care coverage you buy directly from an insurance company, and
- Health care coverage you buy through the Marketplace.

See the instructions for Form 8965 for more information on what qualifies as minimum essential coverage.

Reminder–health care coverage. If you need health care coverage, go to *www.HealthCare.gov* to learn about health insurance options for you and your family, how to buy health insurance, and how you might qualify to get financial assistance to buy health insurance.

Premium tax credit. If you, your spouse, or a dependent enrolled in health insurance through the Marketplace, you may be able to claim the premium tax credit. You must file Form 1040A or 1040 to claim the premium tax credit. See the instructions for Form 8962.

Lines 13a Through 13d

Simple. Safe. Secure.

Fast refunds! Join the eight in 10 taxpayers who choose direct deposit—a fast, simple, safe, secure way to have your refund deposited automatically into your checking or savings account, including an individual retirement arrangement (IRA). For more information about IRAs, see *IRA*, later.

If you want us to directly deposit the amount shown on line 13a to your checking or savings account, including an IRA, at a bank or other financial institution (such as a mutual fund, brokerage firm, or credit union) in the United States:
- Complete lines 13b through 13d (if you want your refund deposited to only one account), or
- Check the box on line 13a and attach Form 8888 if you want to split the direct deposit of your refund into more than one account or use all or part of your refund to buy paper series I savings bonds.

If you do not want your refund directly deposited to your account, do not check the box on line 13a. Draw a line through the boxes on lines 13b and 13d. We will send you a check instead.

Account must be in your name. Don't request a deposit of your refund to an account that isn't in your name, such as your tax return preparer's account. Although you may owe your tax return preparer a fee for preparing your return, don't have any part of your refund deposited into the preparer's account to pay the fee.

The number of refunds that can be directly deposited to a single account or prepaid debit card is limited to three a year. After this limit is reached, paper checks will be sent instead. Learn more at *www.irs.gov/Individuals/Direct-Deposit-Limits*.

Why Use Direct Deposit?
- It is faster. You get your refund faster by direct deposit than you do by check.
- It is more secure. There is no check that can get lost or stolen.
- It is more convenient. You do not have to make a trip to the bank to deposit your check.
- It saves tax dollars. It costs the government less to refund by direct deposit.
- It's proven itself. Nearly 98% of social security and veterans' benefits are sent electronically using direct deposit.

 If you file a joint return and check the box on line 13a and attach Form 8888 or fill in lines 13b through 13d, your spouse may get at least part of the refund.

IRA. You can have your refund (or part of it) directly deposited to a traditional IRA, Roth IRA (including *my*RA), or SEP-IRA, but not a SIMPLE IRA. You must establish the IRA at a bank or other financial institution before you request direct deposit. Make sure your direct deposit will be accepted. You must also notify the trustee or custodian of your account of the year to which the deposit is to be applied (unless the trustee or custodian won't accept a deposit for 2015). If you don't, the trustee or custodian can assume the deposit is for the year during which you are filing the return. For example, if you file your 2015 return during 2016 and do not notify the trustee or custodian in advance, the trustee or custodian can assume the deposit to your IRA is for 2016. If you designate your deposit to be for 2015, you must verify that the deposit was actually made to the account by the due date of the return (not counting extensions). If the deposit isn't made by that date, the deposit isn't an IRA contribution for 2015. If you make a contribution to a traditional IRA for 2015, you may be able to take an IRA deduction, but you must file Form 1040A or 1040 to do so.

 You and your spouse each may be able to contribute up to $5,500 ($6,500 if age 50 or older at the end of 2015) to a traditional IRA or Roth IRA (including myRA) for 2015. You may owe a penalty if your total contributions exceed these limits and the limits may be lower depending on your compensation income. For more information on IRA contributions, see Pub. 590-A. If the limits on IRA contributions change for 2016, Pub. 590-A will have the new 2016 limits.

For more information on IRAs, see Pub. 590-A and Pub. 590-B.

myRA® If you already have a myRA® account, you can request a deposit of your refund (or part of it) to your myRA account. A myRA is a starter retirement account offered by the Department of the Treasury. For more information on myRA and to open a myRA account online, visit *www.myRA.gov*.

TreasuryDirect®. You can request a deposit of your refund (or part of it) to a TreasuryDirect® online account to buy U.S. Treasury marketable securities and savings bonds. For more information, go to *http://go.usa.gov/3KvcP*.

Form 8888. You can have your refund directly deposited into more than one account or use it to buy up to $5,000 in paper series I savings bonds. You do not need a TreasuryDirect® account to do this. For more information, see the Form 8888 instructions.

Line 13a

You cannot file Form 8888 to split your refund into more than one account or buy paper series I savings bonds if Form 8379 is filed with your return.

Line 13b

The routing number must be nine digits. The first two digits must be 01 through 12 or 21 through 32. On the sample check later, the routing number is 250250025. Henry and Naomi Maple would use that routing number unless their financial institution instructed them to use a different routing number for direct deposits.

Ask your financial institution for the correct routing number to enter on line 13b if:
- The routing number on a deposit slip is different from the routing number on your checks,
- Your deposit is to a savings account that doesn't allow you to write checks,

- Your checks state they are payable through a financial institution different from the one at which you have your checking account, or
- Your deposit is to a myRA account.

Line 13c

Check the appropriate box for the type of account. Do not check more than one box. If the deposit is to an account such as an IRA, health savings account, brokerage account, or other similar account, ask your financial institution whether you should check the "Checking" or "Savings" box. You must check the correct box to ensure your deposit is accepted. If your deposit is to a myRA account or TreasuryDirect® online account, check the "Savings" box.

Line 13d

The account number can be up to 17 characters (both numbers and letters). Include hyphens but omit spaces and special symbols. Enter the number from left to right and leave any unused boxes blank. On the sample check below, the account number is 20202086. Do not include the check number.

If the direct deposit to your account(s) is different from the amount you expected, you will receive an explanation in the mail about 2 weeks after your refund is deposited.

Sample Check—Lines 13b Through 13d

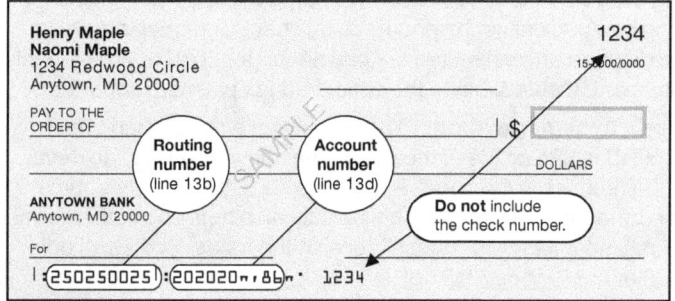

 *The routing and account numbers may be in different places on your check.*

Reasons Your Direct Deposit Request Will Be Rejected

If any of the following apply, your direct deposit request will be rejected and a check will be sent instead.
- You are asking to have a joint refund deposited to an individual account, and your financial institution(s) won't allow this. The IRS isn't responsible if a financial institution rejects a direct deposit.
- The name on your account doesn't match the name on the refund, and your financial institution(s) won't allow a refund to be deposited unless the name on the refund matches the name on the account.
- Three direct deposits of tax refunds have already been made to the same account or prepaid debit card.
- You haven't given a valid account number.
- You file your 2015 return after December 31, 2016.

- Any numbers or letters on lines 13b through 13d are crossed out or whited out.

 The IRS isn't responsible for a lost refund if you enter the wrong account information. Check with your financial institution to get the correct routing and account numbers and to make sure your direct deposit will be accepted.

Amount You Owe

 IRS *e-file* offers two electronic payment options. With Electronic Funds Withdrawal, you can pay your current year balance due and also make up to four estimated tax payments. If you file early, you can schedule your payment for withdrawal from your account on a future date, up to and including the due date of the return. Or you can pay using a debit or credit card. Visit *www.irs.gov/payments* for details on both options.

Line 14, Amount You Owe

 To save interest and penalties, pay your taxes in full by the due date of your return (not counting extensions)—April 18, 2016, for most people. You do not have to pay if line 14 is under $1.

Include any estimated penalty for not paying enough tax during the year (explained later) in the amount you enter on line 14. You can pay online, by phone, or by check or money order. Do not include any estimated tax payments (for 2015 or 2016) in this payment. Instead, make the estimated tax payment separately.

Bad check or payment. The penalty for writing a bad check to the IRS is $25 or 2% of the check, whichever is more. However, if the amount of the check is less than $25, the penalty equals the amount of the check. This penalty also applies to other forms of payment if the IRS doesn't receive the funds. See Tax Topic 206 at *www.irs.gov/taxtopics*.

Pay Online

Paying online is convenient and secure and helps make sure we get your payments on time.

To pay your taxes online or for more information, go to *www.irs.gov/payments*. You can pay using either of the following electronic payment methods.
- *IRS Direct Pay* for online transfers from your checking or savings account.
- Debit or credit card. Click on "Pay by Card."

Also see the *e-file* information under *Amount You Owe*, earlier, for more information about the Electronic Funds Withdrawal payment option offered when e-filing your return.

Pay by Phone

Paying by phone is another safe and secure method of paying electronically. Use one of the following methods.
- Direct transfer using Electronic Federal Tax Payment System (EFTPS).
- Debit or credit card.

Direct transfer. To use EFTPS, you must be enrolled. You can enroll online or have an enrollment form mailed to you. To make a payment using EFTPS, call 1-800-555-4477 (English) or 1-800-244-4829 (Spanish). People who are deaf, hard of hearing, or have a speech disability and who have access to TTY/TDD equipment can call 1-800-733-4829. For more information about EFTPS, go to *www.irs.gov/payments*.

Debit or credit card. To pay using a debit or credit card, you can call one of the following service providers. There is a convenience fee charged by these providers that varies by provider, card type, and payment amount.

Official Payments Corporation
1-888-UPAY-TAX™ (1-888-872-9829)
www.officialpayments.com

Link2Gov Corporation
1-888-PAY-1040™ (1-888-729-1040)
www.PAY1040.com

WorldPay US, Inc.
1-844-PAY-TAX-8™ (1-844-729-8298)
www.payUSAtax.com

For the latest details on how to pay by phone, go to *www.irs.gov/payments*.

Pay by Check or Money Order

Make your check or money order payable to "United States Treasury" for the full amount due. Do not attach the payment to your return. Do not send cash. Write "2015 Form 1040EZ" and your name, address, daytime phone number, and social security number (SSN) on your payment. If you are filing a joint return, enter the SSN shown first on your return.

To help us process your payment, enter the amount on the right side of the check like this: $ XXX.XX. Do not use dashes or lines (for example, do not enter "$XXX–" or "$XXX XX/100").

Then, complete Form 1040-V following the instructions on that form and enclose it in the envelope with your tax return and payment.

 You may need to (a) increase the amount of income tax withheld from your pay by filing a new Form W-4, (b) increase the tax withheld from other income by filing Form W-4V, or (c) make estimated tax payments for 2016. See Income tax withholding and estimated tax payments for 2016 *in Section 5, later.*

What if You Cannot Pay?

If you cannot pay the full amount shown on line 14 when you file, you can ask for:
- An installment agreement, or
- An extension of time to pay.

Installment agreement. Under an installment agreement, you can pay all or part of the tax you owe in monthly installments. However, even if your request to pay in installments is granted, you will be charged interest and may be charged a late payment penalty on the tax not paid by the due date of your return (not counting extensions)–April 18, 2016, for most people. You also must pay a fee. To limit the interest and penalty charges, pay as much of the tax as possible when you file. But before requesting an installment agreement, you should consider other less costly alternatives, such as a bank loan or credit card payment.

To ask for an installment agreement, you can apply online or use Form 9465. To apply online, go to IRS.gov and click on *Apply for an Online Payment Plan*.

Extension of time to pay. If paying the tax when it is due would cause you an undue hardship, you can ask for an extension of time to pay by filing Form 1127 by the due date of your return (not counting extensions)–April 18, 2016, for most people. You will still be charged interest on the tax not paid by April 15, 2016. An extension generally won't be granted for more than 6 months. You must pay the tax before the extension runs out. If you don't, penalties may be imposed.

Penalty for Not Paying Enough Tax During the Year

You may have to pay a penalty if line 14 is at least $1,000 and it is more than 10% of the tax shown on your return. The "tax shown on your return" is the amount on line 10 minus the amount on line 8a. You may choose to have the IRS figure the penalty for you. If you owe a penalty, the IRS will send you a bill. However, if you want to figure the penalty yourself on Form 2210, you must file Form 1040A or 1040 to do so.

The penalty may be waived under certain conditions. See Pub. 505 for details.

Exceptions to the penalty. You won't owe the penalty if your 2014 tax return was for a tax year of 12 full months and either of the following applies.

1. You had no tax shown on your 2014 return and you were a U.S. citizen or resident for all of 2014, or

2. Line 7 on your 2015 return is at least as much as the tax shown on your 2014 return.

Third Party Designee

If you want to allow your preparer, a friend, a family member, or any other person you choose to discuss your 2015 tax return with the IRS, check the "Yes" box in the "Third Party Designee" area of your return. Also, enter the designee's name, phone number, and any five digits the designee chooses as his or her personal identification number (PIN).

If you check the "Yes" box, you, and your spouse if filing a joint return, are authorizing the IRS to call the designee to answer any questions that may arise during the processing of your return. You also are authorizing the designee to:
- Give the IRS any information that is missing from your return,
- Call the IRS for information about the processing of your return or the status of your refund or payment(s),
- Receive copies of notices or transcripts related to your return, upon request, and
- Respond to certain IRS notices about math errors, offsets, and return preparation.

You aren't authorizing the designee to receive any refund check, bind you to anything (including any additional tax liability), or otherwise represent you before the IRS.

The authorization will automatically end no later than the due date (not counting extensions) for filing your 2016 tax return. This is April 18, 2017, for most people.

Signing Your Return

Form 1040EZ isn't considered a valid return unless you sign it. If you are filing a joint return, your spouse also must sign. If your spouse cannot sign the return, see Pub. 501. Be sure to date your return and enter your occupation(s). If you have someone prepare your return, you are still responsible for the correctness of the return. If your return is signed for you by a representative, you must have a power of attorney attached that specifically authorizes the representative to sign your return. To do this, you can use Form 2848. If you are filing a joint return as a surviving spouse, see *Death of a Taxpayer* in Section 1, earlier.

Court-Appointed Conservator, Guardian, or Other Fiduciary. If you are a court-appointed conservator, guardian, or other fiduciary for a mentally or physically incompetent individual who has to file Form 1040EZ, sign your name for the individual. You should also file Form 56, Notice Concerning Fiduciary Relationship, when you first begin those duties for the individual.

Child's return. If your child cannot sign his or her return, either parent can sign the child's name in the space provided. Then, add "By (your signature), parent for minor child."

Daytime phone number. Providing your daytime phone number may help speed the processing of your return. We may have questions about items on your return, such as the earned income credit. If you answer our questions over the phone, we may be able to continue processing your return without mailing you a letter. If you are filing a joint return, you can enter either your or your spouse's daytime phone number.

Identity protection PIN. For 2015, if you received an IRS notice providing you with an Identity Protection Personal Identification Number (IP PIN), enter it in the IP PIN spaces provided below your daytime phone number. You must correctly enter all six numbers of your IP PIN. If you didn't receive a notice containing an IP PIN, leave these spaces blank.

 New IP PINs are issued every year. Enter the latest IP PIN you received. IP PINs for 2015 tax returns generally were sent in December 2015.

If you are filing a joint return and both taxpayers receive an IP PIN, only the taxpayer whose social security number (SSN) appears first on the tax return should enter his or her IP PIN. However, if you are filing electronically, both taxpayers must enter their IP PINs.

If you need more information, go to *www.irs.gov/Individuals/ Understanding-Your-CP01A-Notice*. If you received an IP PIN but misplaced it, call 1-800-908-4490.

Paid preparer must sign your return. Generally, anyone you pay to prepare your return must sign it and include their preparer tax identification number (PTIN) in the space provided. The preparer must give you a copy of the return for your records.

Someone who prepares your return but doesn't charge you should not sign your return.

 Electronic return signatures! To file your return electronically, you must sign the return electronically using a personal identification number (PIN). If you are filing online using software, you must use a Self-Select PIN. If you are filing electronically using a tax practitioner, you can use a Self-Select PIN or a Practitioner PIN.

Self-Select PIN. The Self-Select PIN method allows you to create your own PIN. If you are filing a joint return, both you and your spouse must create a separate PIN to enter as an electronic signature.

A PIN is any combination of five digits you choose except five zeros. If you use a PIN, there is nothing to sign and nothing to mail—not even your Forms W-2.

To verify your identity, you will be prompted to enter your adjusted gross income (AGI) from your originally filed 2014 federal income tax return, if applicable. Do not use your AGI from an amended return (Form 1040X) or a math error correction made by the IRS. AGI is the amount shown on your 2014 Form 1040, line 38; Form 1040A, line 22; or Form 1040EZ, line 4. If you do not have your 2014 income tax return, call the IRS at 1-800-908-9946 to get a free transcript of your return or visit *www.irs.gov/Individuals/Get-Transcript*. (If you filed electronically last year, you may use your prior year PIN to verify your identity instead of your prior year AGI. The prior year PIN is the five digit PIN you used to electronically sign your 2014 return.) You also will be prompted to enter your date of birth (DOB).

 You cannot use the Self-Select PIN method if you are a first-time filer under age 16 at the end of 2015.

If you cannot locate your prior year AGI or prior year PIN, use the Electronic Filing PIN Request. *This can be found at* IRS.gov. *Click on "Request an Electronic Filing PIN." Or you can call 1-866-704-7388.*

Practitioner PIN. The Practitioner PIN method allows you to authorize your tax practitioner to enter or generate your PIN. The practitioner can provide you with details.

Form 8453. You must send in a paper Form 8453 if you are attaching or filing Form 2848 (for an electronic return signed by an agent).

Section 4—After You Have Finished

Return Checklist

This checklist can help you file a correct return. Mistakes can delay your refund or result in notices being sent to you. One of the best ways to file an accurate return is to file electronically. Tax software does the math for you and will help you avoid mistakes. You may be eligible to use free tax software that will take the guesswork out of preparing your return. Free File makes available free brand-name software and free *e-file*. Visit *www.irs.gov/freefile* for details. Join the eight in 10 taxpayers who get their refunds faster by using direct deposit and *e-file*.

Did you:

☐ Enter the correct social security number for you and your spouse, if married, in the space provided on Form 1040EZ? Check that your name and SSN agree with your social security card.

☐ Use the amount from line 6, and the proper filing status, to find your tax in the Tax Table? Be sure you entered the correct tax on line 10.

☐ Go through the three steps in the instructions for lines 8a and 8b, if you thought you could take the EIC? If you could take the EIC, did you take special care to use the proper filing status column in the EIC Table?

☐ Check your math, especially when figuring your taxable income, federal income tax withheld, earned income credit, total payments, and your refund or amount you owe?

☐ Check one or both boxes on line 5 if you (or your spouse) can be claimed as a dependent on someone's (such as your parents') 2015 return? Did you check the box even if that person chooses not to claim you (or your spouse)? Did you leave the boxes blank if no one can claim you (or your spouse) as a dependent?

☐ Enter an amount on line 5? If you checked any of the boxes, did you use the worksheet on the back of Form 1040EZ to figure the amount to enter? If you did not check any of the boxes, did you enter $10,300 if single; $20,600 if married filing jointly?

☐ Sign and date Form 1040EZ and enter your occupation(s)?

☐ Include your apartment number in your address if you live in an apartment?

☐ Attach your Form(s) W-2 to the left margin of Form 1040EZ?

☐ Include all the required information on your payment if you owe tax and are paying by check or money order? See the instructions for line 14 in Section 3, earlier.

☐ File only one original return for the same year, even if you have not gotten your refund or have not heard from the IRS since you filed? Filing more than one original return for the same year or sending in more than one copy of the same return (unless we ask you to do so) could delay your refund.

Filing the Return

Due Date

File Form 1040EZ by **April 18, 2016**. The due date is April 18, instead of April 15, because of the Emancipation Day holiday in the District of Columbia—even if you do not live in the District of Columbia. If you live in Maine or Massachusetts, you have until April 19, 2016. That is because of the Patriots' Day holiday in those states. If you file after this date, you may have to pay interest and penalties, discussed later in this Section 4.

If you were serving in, or in support of, the U.S. Armed Forces in a designated combat zone or a contingency operation, you may be able to file later. See Pub. 3 for details.

What if You Cannot File on Time?

You can get an automatic 6-month extension to file your return if, no later than the date your return is due, you file Form 4868. For details, see Form 4868. Instead of filing Form 4868, you can apply for an automatic extension by making an electronic payment by the due date of your return.

 An automatic 6-month extension to file doesn't extend the time to pay your tax. If you do not pay your tax by the original due date of your return, you will owe interest on the unpaid tax and may owe penalties. See Form 4868.

If you make a payment with your extension request, see the instructions for line 9 in Section 3, earlier.

What if You File or Pay Late?

We can charge you interest and penalties on the amount you owe.

Interest. We will charge you interest on taxes not paid by their due date, even if an extension of time to file is granted. We will also charge you interest on penalties imposed for failure to file, negligence, fraud, substantial valuation misstatements, substantial understatements of tax, and reportable transaction understatements. Interest is charged on the penalty from the due date of the return (including extensions).

Penalties

Late filing. If you do not file your return by the due date (including extensions), the penalty is usually 5% of the amount due for each month or part of a month your return is late, unless you have a reasonable explanation. If you do, include it with your return. The penalty can be as much as 25% of the tax due. The penalty is 15% per month, up to a maximum of 75%, if the failure to file is fraudulent. If your return is more than 60 days late, the minimum penalty could be as much as the amount of any tax you owe.

Late payment of tax. If you pay your taxes late, the penalty is usually ½ of 1% of the unpaid amount for each month or part of a month the tax isn't paid. The penalty can be as much as 25% of the unpaid amount. It applies to any unpaid tax on the return. This penalty is in addition to interest charges on late payments.

Frivolous return. In addition to any other penalties, there is a penalty of $5,000 for filing a frivolous return. A frivolous return is one that doesn't contain information needed to figure the correct tax or shows a substantially incorrect tax because you take a frivolous position or desire to delay or interfere with the tax laws. This includes altering or striking out the preprinted language above the space where you sign. For a list of positions identified as frivolous, see Notice 2010-33, which is on page 609 of Internal Revenue Bulletin 2010-17 at *www.irs.gov/pub/irs-irbs/ irb10-17.pdf*.

Are there other penalties? Yes. There are penalties for negligence, substantial understatement of tax, reportable transaction understatements, filing an erroneous refund claim, and fraud. Criminal penalties may be imposed for willful failure to file, tax evasion, making a false statement, or identity theft. See Pub. 17 for details.

Where Do You File?

If you e-file your return, there is no need to mail it. See the e-file page earlier or IRS.gov for more information. However, if you choose to mail it, filing instructions and addresses are at the end of these instructions.

Private delivery services. If you choose to mail your return, you can use only the following IRS-designated private delivery services to meet the "timely mailing treated as timely filing/ paying" rule for tax returns and payments.

- FedEx First Overnight, FedEx Priority Overnight, FedEx Standard Overnight, FedEx 2 Day, FedEx International Next Flight Out, FedEx International Priority, FedEx International First, and FedEx International Economy.
- UPS Next Day Air Early AM, UPS Next Day Air, UPS Next Day Air Saver, UPS 2nd Day Air, UPS 2nd Day Air A.M., UPS Worldwide Express Plus, and UPS Worldwide Express.

For more information, go to IRS.gov and enter "private delivery service" in the search box. The search results will direct you to the IRS mailing address to use if you are using a private delivery service. You will also find any updates to the list of designated private delivery services. The private delivery service can tell you how to get written proof of the mailing date.

Section 5—General Information

The IRS Mission. Provide America's taxpayers top-quality service by helping them understand and meet their tax responsibilities and enforce the law with integrity and fairness to all.

Income tax withholding and estimated tax payments for 2016. If the amount you owe or your refund is large, you may want to file a new Form W-4 with your employer to change the amount of income tax withheld from your 2016 pay. For details on how to complete Form W-4, see Pub. 505. If you receive certain government payments (such as unemployment compensation or social security benefits), you can have tax withheld from those payments by giving the payer Form W-4V.

 You can use the IRS Withholding Calculator at www.irs.gov/Individuals/IRS-Withholding-Calculator, instead of Pub. 505 or the worksheets included with Form W-4 or W-4P, to determine whether you need to have your withholding increased or decreased.

In general, you do not have to make estimated tax payments if you expect that your 2016 tax return will show a tax refund or a tax balance due of less than $1,000. See Pub. 505 for more details.

Secure your records from identity theft. Identity theft occurs when someone uses your personal information, such as your name, social security number (SSN), or other identifying information, without your permission, to commit fraud or other crimes. An identity thief may use your SSN to get a job or may file a tax return using your SSN to receive a refund.

To reduce your risk:
● Protect your SSN,
● Ensure your employer is protecting your SSN, and
● Be careful when choosing a tax preparer.

If your tax records are affected by identity theft and you receive a notice from the IRS, respond right away to the name and phone number printed on the IRS notice or letter. For more information, see Pub. 4535.

If your tax records aren't currently affected by identity theft but you think you are at risk due to a lost or stolen purse or wallet, questionable credit card activity or credit report, etc., visit www.irs.gov/identitytheft to learn what steps you should take.

Victims of identity theft who are experiencing economic harm or a systemic problem, or are seeking help in resolving tax problems that haven't been resolved through normal channels, may be eligible for Taxpayer Advocate Service (TAS) assistance. You can reach TAS by calling the National Taxpayer Advocate Helpline at 1-877-777-4778. People who are deaf, hard of hearing, or have a speech disability and who have access to TTY/TDD equipment can call 1-800-829-4059. Deaf or hard of hearing individuals can also contact the IRS through relay services such as the Federal Relay Service available at www.gsa.gov/fedrelay.

Protect yourself from suspicious emails or phishing schemes. Phishing is the creation and use of email and websites designed to mimic legitimate business emails and websites. The most common form is sending an email to a user falsely claiming to be an established legitimate enterprise in an attempt to scam the user into surrendering private information that will be used for identity theft.

The IRS doesn't initiate contacts with taxpayers via emails. Also, the IRS doesn't request detailed personal information through email or ask taxpayers for the PIN numbers, passwords, or similar secret access information for their credit card, bank, or other financial accounts.

If you receive an unsolicited email claiming to be from the IRS, forward the message to phishing@irs.gov. You may also report misuse of the IRS name, logo, forms, or other IRS property to the Treasury Inspector General for Tax Administration toll-free at 1-800-366-4484. People who are deaf, hard of hearing, or have a speech disability and who have access to TTY/TDD equipment can call 1-800-877-8339.

You can forward suspicious emails to the Federal Trade Commission at spam@uce.gov or contact them at www.ftc.gov/idtheft or 1-877-IDTHEFT (1-877-438-4338). People who are deaf, hard of hearing, or have a speech disability and who have access to TTY/TDD equipment can call 1-866-653-4261.

Visit IRS.gov and enter "identity theft" in the search box to learn more about identity theft and how to reduce your risk.

How Long Should Records Be Kept? Keep a copy of your tax return, worksheets you used, and records of all items appearing on it (such as Forms W-2 and 1099) until the statute of limitations runs out for that return. Usually, this is 3 years from the date the return was due or filed or 2 years from the date the tax was paid, whichever is later. You should keep some records longer. For more details, see chapter 1 of Pub. 17.

Amended Return File Form 1040X to change a return you already filed. Generally, Form 1040X must be filed within 3 years after the date the original return was filed or within 2 years after the date the tax was paid, whichever is later. But you may have more time to file Form 1040X if you live in a federally declared disaster area or you are physically or mentally unable to manage your financial affairs. See Pub. 556 for details.

Use the "Where's My Amended Return" application on IRS.gov to track the status of your amended return. It can take up to 3 weeks from the date you mailed it to show up in our system.

Need a Copy of Your Tax Return Information? Tax return transcripts are free and are generally used to validate income and tax filing status for mortgage applications, student and small business loan applications, and during tax preparation. To get a free transcript:
● Visit www.irs.gov/Individuals/Get-Transcript
● Use Form 4506-T or 4506T-EZ, or
● Call us at 1-800-908-9946.

If you need a copy of your actual tax return, use Form 4506. There is a fee for each return requested. See Form 4506 for the current fee. If your main home, principal place of business, or tax records are located in a federally declared disaster area, this fee will be waived.

Past due returns. If you or someone you know needs to file past due tax returns, see Tax Topic 153 at www.irs.gov/taxtopics or visit www.irs.gov/individuals for help in filing those returns. Send the returns to the address that applies to you in the latest Form 1040EZ instructions. For example, if you are filing a 2012 return in 2016, use the address at the end of these instructions. However, if you got an IRS notice, mail the return to the address in the notice.

Innocent spouse relief. Generally, both you and your spouse are each responsible for paying the full amount of tax, interest, and penalties on your joint return. However, you may qualify for relief from liability for tax on a joint return if (a) there is an understatement of tax because your spouse omitted income or claimed false deductions or credits, (b) you are divorced, separated, or no longer living with your spouse, or (c) given all the facts and circumstances, it wouldn't be fair to hold you liable for the tax. File Form 8857 to request relief. In some cases, Form 8857 may need to be filed within 2 years of the date on which the IRS first attempted to collect the tax from you. Do not file Form 8857 with your Form 1040EZ. For more information, see Pub. 971 and Form 8857 or you can call the Innocent Spouse office toll-free at 1-855-851-2009.

How do you make a gift to reduce debt held by the public?

If you wish to do so, make a check payable to "Bureau of the Fiscal Service." You can send it to:

Bureau of the Fiscal Service
Attn Dept G
P.O. Box 2188
Parkersburg, WV 26106-2188

Or you can enclose the check with your income tax return when you file. In the memo section of the check, note that it is a gift to reduce the debt held by the public. Do not add your gift to any tax you may owe. See the instructions for line 14 for details on how to pay any tax you owe.

For information on how to make this gift online, go to *www.treasurydirect.gov* and click on "How To Make a Contribution to Reduce the Debt."

 You may be able to deduct this gift on your 2016 tax return.

The Taxpayer Advocate Service Is Here To Help You

What is the Taxpayer Advocate Service?

The Taxpayer Advocate Service (TAS) is an *independent* organization within the Internal Revenue Service (IRS) that helps taxpayers and protects taxpayer rights. Our job is to ensure that every taxpayer is treated fairly and that you know and understand your rights under the *Taxpayer Bill of Rights*.

What can the Taxpayer Advocate Service do for you?

We can help you resolve problems that you can't resolve with the IRS. And our service is free. If you qualify for our assistance, your advocate will be with you at every turn and do everything possible. TAS can help you if:

- Your problem is causing financial difficulty for you, your family, or your business.

- You face (or your business is facing) an immediate threat of adverse action.
- You've tried repeatedly to contact the IRS but no one has responded, or the IRS hasn't responded by the date promised.

How can you reach us?

We have offices in *every state, the District of Columbia, and Puerto Rico*. Your local advocate's number is at *TaxpayerAdvocate.irs.gov*, at *www.irs.gov/advocate*, and in your local directory. You can also call us toll-free at 1-877-777-4778.

How can you learn about your taxpayer rights?

The Taxpayer Bill of Rights describes ten basic rights that all taxpayers have when dealing with the IRS. Our Tax Toolkit at *TaxpayerAdvocate.irs.gov* can help you understand *what these rights mean to you* and how they apply. These are **your** rights. Know them. Use them.

How else does the Taxpayer Advocate Service help taxpayers?

TAS works to resolve large-scale problems that affect many taxpayers. If you know of one of these broad issues, please report it to us at *www.irs.gov/sams*.

Low Income Taxpayer Clinics Help Taxpayers

Low Income Taxpayer Clinics (LITCs) are independent from the IRS. Some serve individuals whose income is below a certain level and who need to resolve a tax problem. These clinics provide professional representation before the IRS or in court on audits, appeals, tax collection disputes, and other issues for free or for a small fee. Some clinics provide information about taxpayer rights and responsibilities in many different languages for individuals who speak English as a second language. For more information, and to find a clinic near you, read the LITC page on *www.irs.gov/litc* or Pub. 4134, Low Income Taxpayer Clinic List. You can get this publication at your local IRS office or by calling 1-800-829-3676.

Suggestions for Improving the IRS
Taxpayer Advocacy Panel

Have a suggestion for improving the IRS and do not know who to contact? The Taxpayer Advocacy Panel (TAP) is a diverse group of citizen volunteers who listen to taxpayers, identify taxpayers' issues, and make suggestions for improving IRS service and customer satisfaction. The panel is demographically and geographically diverse, with at least one member from each state, the District of Columbia, and Puerto Rico. Contact TAP at *www.improveirs.org* or 1-888-912-1227 (toll-free).

Section 6—How To Get Tax Help

Do you need help with a tax issue or preparing your tax return, or do you need a free publication or form?

Getting answers to your tax law questions. *IRS.gov* and IRS2Go are ready when you are—24 hours a day, 7 days a week.

- Enter "ITA" in the search box on *IRS.gov* for the Interactive Tax Assistant, a tool that will ask you questions on a number of tax law topics and provide answers. You can print the entire interview and the final response.
- Enter "Pub 17" in the search box to get Pub. 17, Your Federal Income Tax for Individuals, which features details on tax-saving opportunities, 2015 tax changes, and thousands of interactive links to help you find answers to your questions.
- Access tax law information in your electronic filing software.
- Go to *www.irs.gov/Help-&-Resources* for a variety of tools that will help you with your taxes.

Preparing and filing your tax return. Find free options to prepare and file your return on IRS.gov or in your local community if you qualify.

- Go to IRS.gov and click on the Filing tab to see your options.
- Enter "Free File" in the search box to see whether you can use brand name software to prepare and e-file your federal tax return for free.
- Enter "VITA" in the search box, download the free IRS2Go app, or call 1-800-906- 9887 to find the nearest Volunteer Income Tax Assistance or Tax Counseling for the Elderly (TCE) location for free tax preparation.
- Enter "TCE" in the search box, download the free IRS2Go app, or call 1-888-227- 7669 to find the nearest Tax Counseling for the Elderly location for free tax preparation.

In general, the Volunteer Income Tax Assistance (VITA) program offers free tax help to people who make $54,000 or less, persons with disabilities, the elderly, and limited- English-speaking taxpayers who need help preparing their own tax returns. The Tax Counseling for the Elderly (TCE) program offers free tax help for all taxpayers, particularly those who are 60 years of age and older. TCE volunteers specialize in answering questions about pensions and retirement-related issues unique to seniors.

Tax forms and publications. You can download or print all of the forms and publications you may need on *IRS.gov/ formspubs*. Otherwise, you can:

- Go to *IRS.gov/formspubs* to place an order and have forms mailed to you, or
- Call 1-800-829-3676 to order current-year forms, instructions, publications, and prior-year forms and instructions (limited to 5 years).

You should receive your order within 10 business days.

Where to file your tax return.

- Remember, there are many ways to file your return electronically. It's safe, quick and easy. See *Preparing and filing your tax return*, above, for more information.
- See *Where Do You File?* at the end of these instructions to determine where to mail your completed paper tax return.

Getting a transcript or copy of a return.

- Go to *www.irs.gov/Individuals/Get-Transcript*.
- Download the free IRS2Go app to your smart phone and use it to order transcripts of your tax returns or tax account.
- Call the transcript toll-free line: 1-800-908-9946.
- Mail Form 4506-T or Form 4506T-EZ (both available on IRS.gov).

Using online tools to help prepare your return. Go to *IRS.gov* and click on the Tools bar to use these and other self-service options.

- The *Earned Income Tax Credit Assistant* determines if you're eligible for the EIC.
- The *IRS Withholding Calculator* estimates the amount you should have withheld from your paycheck for federal income tax purposes.
- The *Electronic Filing PIN Request* helps to verify your identity when you do not have your prior year AGI or prior self-selected PIN available.

Understanding identity theft issues.

- Go to *irs.gov/uac/Identity-Protection* for information and videos.
- See *Secure your records from identity theft* under *General Information*, earlier.

Checking on the status of a refund.

- Go to *IRS.gov/refunds*.
- Download the free IRS2Go app to your smart phone and use it to check your refund status.
- Call the automated refund hotline: 1-800-829-1954. See *Refund Information*, later.

Making a tax payment. The IRS uses the latest encryption technology so electronic payments are safe and secure. You can make electronic payments online, by phone, or from a mobile device. Paying electronically is quick, easy, and faster than mailing in a check or money order. Go to *www.IRS.gov/payments* to make a payment using any of the following options.

- *IRS Direct Pay* (for individual taxpayers who have a checking or savings account).
- **Debit or credit card** (approved payment processors online or by phone).
- **Electronic Funds Withdrawal** (available during *e-file*).
- **Check or money order**.

IRS2Go provides access to mobile-friendly payment options like IRS Direct Pay, offering you a free, secure way to pay directly from your bank account. You can also make debit or credit card payments through an approved payment processor. Simply download IRS2Go from Google Play, the Apple App Store, or the Amazon Appstore, and make your payments anytime, anywhere.

What if I can't pay now? Click on the Payments tab or the "Pay Your Tax Bill" icon on IRS.gov for more information about these additional options.

- Apply for an *online payment agreement* to meet your tax obligations in monthly installments if you can't pay your taxes in full today. Once you complete the online process, you will receive immediate notification of whether your agreement has been approved.
- An offer in compromise allows you to settle your tax debt for less than the full amount you owe. Use the *Offer in Compromise Pre-Qualifier* to confirm your eligibility.

Checking the status of an amended return.

- Go to IRS.gov and click on the Tools tab and then *Where's My Amended Return?*

Understanding an IRS notice or letter.

- Enter "Understanding your notice" in the search box on IRS.gov to find additional information about your IRS notice or letter.

Visiting the IRS. Locate the nearest Taxpayer Assistance Center using the Office Locator tool on *IRS.gov*. Enter "office locator" in the search box. Or choose the "Contact Us" option on the IRS2Go app and search Local Offices. Before you visit, use the Locator tool to check hours and services available.

Watching IRS videos. The IRS Video portal contains video and audio presentations on topics of interest to individuals, small businesses, and tax professionals. You'll find video clips of tax topics, archived versions of live panel discussions and Webinars, and audio archives of tax practitioner phone forums.

Getting tax Information in other languages. For taxpayers whose native language isn't English, we have the following resources available.

- Spanish – *www.irs.gov/Spanish*
- Chinese – *www.irs.gov/Chinese*
- Korean – *www.irs.gov/Korean*
- Vietnamese – *www.irs.gov/Vietnamese*
- Russian – *www.irs.gov/Russian*

- Over-the-phone interpreter service - The IRS Taxpayer Assistance Centers provide telephone interpreter service in over 170 languages, and the service is available free to taxpayers.

Online ordering of tax forms and publications. To order tax forms and publications delivered by mail, go to *www.irs.gov/formspubs* and click on "Order Forms & Pubs." For current year tax forms and publications, click on "Forms and Publications by Mail."

Refund Information

 *where's my refund?*

Information about your return will generally be available within 24 hours after the IRS receives your e-filed return, or 4 weeks after you mail a paper return. But if you filed Form 8379 with your return, allow 14 weeks (11 weeks if you filed electronically) before checking your refund status.

 Visit IRS.gov and click on *Where's My Refund*, or use the free IRS2GO app, 24 hours a day, 7 days a week.

To use *Where's My Refund?* have a copy of your tax return handy. You will need to enter the following information from your return:

- Your social security number (or individual taxpayer identification number),
- Your filing status, and
- The exact whole dollar amount of your refund.

Where's My Refund? will provide an actual personalized refund date as soon as the IRS processes your tax return and approves your refund.

Where's My Refund? doesn't track refunds that are claimed on an amended tax return.

 Updates to refund status are made no more than once a day—usually at night.

 If you do not have Internet access, call 1-800-829-1954 24 hours a day, 7 days a week, for automated refund information.

Note. Our phone and walk-in assistors can research the status of your refund only if it's been 21 days or more since you filed electronically or more than 6 weeks since you mailed your paper return.

Do not send in a copy of your return unless asked to do so.

To get a refund, you generally must file your return within 3 years from the date the return was due (including extensions).

Refund information also is available in Spanish at *www.irs.gov/Spanish* and the phone number listed above.

Tax Topics

Tax Topics is a wide-ranging directory of tax information that is available anytime. You can read these Tax Topics at *www.irs.gov/taxtopics*.

Taxpayer Bill of Rights

All taxpayers have fundamental rights they should be aware of when dealing with the IRS. The Taxpayer Bill of Rights, which the IRS adopted in June of 2014, takes existing rights in the tax code and groups them into the following 10 broad categories, making them easier to understand. Explore your rights and our obligations to protect them.

The right to be informed. Taxpayers have the right to know what they need to do to comply with the tax laws. They are entitled to clear explanations of the laws and IRS procedures in all tax forms, instructions, publications, notices, and correspondence. They have the right to be informed of IRS decisions about their tax accounts and to receive clear explanations of the outcomes.

The right to quality service. Taxpayers have the right to receive prompt, courteous, and professional assistance in their dealings with the IRS, to be spoken to in a way they can easily understand, to receive clear and easily understandable communications from the IRS, and to speak to a supervisor about inadequate service.

The right to pay no more than the correct amount of tax. Taxpayers have the right to pay only the amount of tax legally due, including interest and penalties, and to have the IRS apply all tax payments properly.

The right to challenge the IRS's position and be heard. Taxpayers have the right to raise objections and provide additional documentation in response to formal IRS actions or proposed actions, to expect that the IRS will consider their timely objections and documentation promptly and fairly, and to receive a response if the IRS does not agree with their position.

The right to appeal an IRS decision in an independent forum. Taxpayers are entitled to a fair and impartial administrative appeal of most IRS decisions, including many penalties, and have the right to receive a written response regarding the Office of Appeals' decision. Taxpayers generally have the right to take their cases to court.

The right to finality. Taxpayers have the right to know the maximum amount of time they have to challenge the IRS's position as well as the maximum amount of time the IRS has to audit a particular tax year or collect a tax debt. Taxpayers have the right to know when the IRS has finished an audit.

The right to privacy. Taxpayers have the right to expect that any IRS inquiry, examination, or enforcement action will comply with the law and be no more intrusive than necessary, and will respect all due process rights, including search and seizure protections and will provide, where applicable, a collection due process hearing.

The right to confidentiality. Taxpayers have the right to expect that any information they provide to the IRS will not be disclosed unless authorized by the taxpayer or by law. Taxpayers have the right to expect appropriate action will be taken against employees, return preparers, and others who wrongfully use or disclose taxpayer return information.

The right to retain representation. Taxpayers have the right to retain an authorized representative of their choice to represent them in their dealings with the IRS. Taxpayers have the right to seek assistance from a _Low Income Taxpayer Clinic_ if they cannot afford representation.

The right to a fair and just tax system. Taxpayers have the right to expect the tax system to consider facts and circumstances that might affect their underlying liabilities, ability to pay, or ability to provide information timely. Taxpayers have the right to receive assistance from the _Taxpayer Advocate Service_ if they are experiencing financial difficulty or if the IRS has not resolved their tax issues properly and timely through its normal channels.

Learn more at _www.irs.gov/taxpayerrights_.

2015 Tax Table

Example. Mr. Brown is single. His **taxable income** on line 6 of Form 1040EZ is $26,250. He follows two easy steps to figure his tax: **1.** He finds the $26,250-26,300 taxable income line. **2.** He finds the Single filing status column and reads down the column. The **tax** amount shown where the taxable income line and the filing status line meet is $3,480. He enters this amount on line 10 of Form 1040EZ.

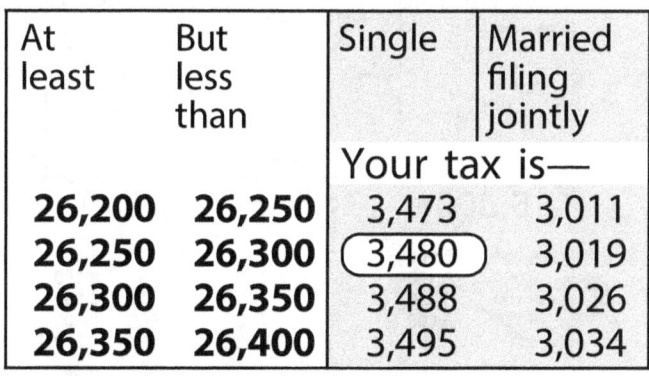

At least	But less than	Single	Married filing jointly
		Your tax is—	
26,200	26,250	3,473	3,011
26,250	26,300	3,480	3,019
26,300	26,350	3,488	3,026
26,350	26,400	3,495	3,034

If Form 1040EZ, line 6, is—		And you are—		If Form 1040EZ, line 6, is—		And you are—		If Form 1040EZ, line 6, is—		And you are—		If Form 1040EZ, line 6, is—		And you are—	
At least	But less than	Single	Married filing jointly	At least	But less than	Single	Married filing jointly	At least	But less than	Single	Married filing jointly	At least	But less than	Single	Married filing jointly
		Your tax is–				Your tax is–				Your tax is–				Your tax is–	
0	5	0	0	**1,000**				**2,000**				**3,000**			
5	15	1	1												
15	25	2	2	1,000	1,025	101	101	2,000	2,025	201	201	3,000	3,050	303	303
25	50	4	4	1,025	1,050	104	104	2,025	2,050	204	204	3,050	3,100	308	308
50	75	6	6	1,050	1,075	106	106	2,050	2,075	206	206	3,100	3,150	313	313
75	100	9	9	1,075	1,100	109	109	2,075	2,100	209	209	3,150	3,200	318	318
100	125	11	11	1,100	1,125	111	111	2,100	2,125	211	211	3,200	3,250	323	323
125	150	14	14												
150	175	16	16	1,125	1,150	114	114	2,125	2,150	214	214	3,250	3,300	328	328
175	200	19	19	1,150	1,175	116	116	2,150	2,175	216	216	3,300	3,350	333	333
				1,175	1,200	119	119	2,175	2,200	219	219	3,350	3,400	338	338
200	225	21	21	1,200	1,225	121	121	2,200	2,225	221	221	3,400	3,450	343	343
225	250	24	24	1,225	1,250	124	124	2,225	2,250	224	224	3,450	3,500	348	348
250	275	26	26												
275	300	29	29	1,250	1,275	126	126	2,250	2,275	226	226	3,500	3,550	353	353
300	325	31	31	1,275	1,300	129	129	2,275	2,300	229	229	3,550	3,600	358	358
				1,300	1,325	131	131	2,300	2,325	231	231	3,600	3,650	363	363
325	350	34	34	1,325	1,350	134	134	2,325	2,350	234	234	3,650	3,700	368	368
350	375	36	36	1,350	1,375	136	136	2,350	2,375	236	236	3,700	3,750	373	373
375	400	39	39												
400	425	41	41	1,375	1,400	139	139	2,375	2,400	239	239	3,750	3,800	378	378
425	450	44	44	1,400	1,425	141	141	2,400	2,425	241	241	3,800	3,850	383	383
				1,425	1,450	144	144	2,425	2,450	244	244	3,850	3,900	388	388
450	475	46	46	1,450	1,475	146	146	2,450	2,475	246	246	3,900	3,950	393	393
475	500	49	49	1,475	1,500	149	149	2,475	2,500	249	249	3,950	4,000	398	398
500	525	51	51												
525	550	54	54	1,500	1,525	151	151	2,500	2,525	251	251	**4,000**			
550	575	56	56	1,525	1,550	154	154	2,525	2,550	254	254				
				1,550	1,575	156	156	2,550	2,575	256	256	4,000	4,050	403	403
575	600	59	59	1,575	1,600	159	159	2,575	2,600	259	259	4,050	4,100	408	408
600	625	61	61	1,600	1,625	161	161	2,600	2,625	261	261	4,100	4,150	413	413
625	650	64	64									4,150	4,200	418	418
650	675	66	66	1,625	1,650	164	164	2,625	2,650	264	264	4,200	4,250	423	423
675	700	69	69	1,650	1,675	166	166	2,650	2,675	266	266	4,250	4,300	428	428
				1,675	1,700	169	169	2,675	2,700	269	269	4,300	4,350	433	433
700	725	71	71	1,700	1,725	171	171	2,700	2,725	271	271	4,350	4,400	438	438
725	750	74	74	1,725	1,750	174	174	2,725	2,750	274	274	4,400	4,450	443	443
750	775	76	76									4,450	4,500	448	448
775	800	79	79	1,750	1,775	176	176	2,750	2,775	276	276	4,500	4,550	453	453
800	825	81	81	1,775	1,800	179	179	2,775	2,800	279	279	4,550	4,600	458	458
				1,800	1,825	181	181	2,800	2,825	281	281	4,600	4,650	463	463
825	850	84	84	1,825	1,850	184	184	2,825	2,850	284	284	4,650	4,700	468	468
850	875	86	86	1,850	1,875	186	186	2,850	2,875	286	286	4,700	4,750	473	473
875	900	89	89												
900	925	91	91	1,875	1,900	189	189	2,875	2,900	289	289	4,750	4,800	478	478
925	950	94	94	1,900	1,925	191	191	2,900	2,925	291	291	4,800	4,850	483	483
				1,925	1,950	194	194	2,925	2,950	294	294	4,850	4,900	488	488
950	975	96	96	1,950	1,975	196	196	2,950	2,975	296	296	4,900	4,950	493	493
975	1,000	99	99	1,975	2,000	199	199	2,975	3,000	299	299	4,950	5,000	498	498

(Continued)

Instructions for Form 1040EZ

If Form 1040EZ, line 6, is–		And you are–	
At least	But less than	Single	Married filing jointly
		Your tax is–	

5,000

At least	But less than	Single	Married filing jointly
5,000	5,050	503	503
5,050	5,100	508	508
5,100	5,150	513	513
5,150	5,200	518	518
5,200	5,250	523	523
5,250	5,300	528	528
5,300	5,350	533	533
5,350	5,400	538	538
5,400	5,450	543	543
5,450	5,500	548	548
5,500	5,550	553	553
5,550	5,600	558	558
5,600	5,650	563	563
5,650	5,700	568	568
5,700	5,750	573	573
5,750	5,800	578	578
5,800	5,850	583	583
5,850	5,900	588	588
5,900	5,950	593	593
5,950	6,000	598	598

6,000

At least	But less than	Single	Married filing jointly
6,000	6,050	603	603
6,050	6,100	608	608
6,100	6,150	613	613
6,150	6,200	618	618
6,200	6,250	623	623
6,250	6,300	628	628
6,300	6,350	633	633
6,350	6,400	638	638
6,400	6,450	643	643
6,450	6,500	648	648
6,500	6,550	653	653
6,550	6,600	658	658
6,600	6,650	663	663
6,650	6,700	668	668
6,700	6,750	673	673
6,750	6,800	678	678
6,800	6,850	683	683
6,850	6,900	688	688
6,900	6,950	693	693
6,950	7,000	698	698

7,000

At least	But less than	Single	Married filing jointly
7,000	7,050	703	703
7,050	7,100	708	708
7,100	7,150	713	713
7,150	7,200	718	718
7,200	7,250	723	723
7,250	7,300	728	728
7,300	7,350	733	733
7,350	7,400	738	738
7,400	7,450	743	743
7,450	7,500	748	748
7,500	7,550	753	753
7,550	7,600	758	758
7,600	7,650	763	763
7,650	7,700	768	768
7,700	7,750	773	773
7,750	7,800	778	778
7,800	7,850	783	783
7,850	7,900	788	788
7,900	7,950	793	793
7,950	8,000	798	798

8,000

At least	But less than	Single	Married filing jointly
8,000	8,050	803	803
8,050	8,100	808	808
8,100	8,150	813	813
8,150	8,200	818	818
8,200	8,250	823	823
8,250	8,300	828	828
8,300	8,350	833	833
8,350	8,400	838	838
8,400	8,450	843	843
8,450	8,500	848	848
8,500	8,550	853	853
8,550	8,600	858	858
8,600	8,650	863	863
8,650	8,700	868	868
8,700	8,750	873	873
8,750	8,800	878	878
8,800	8,850	883	883
8,850	8,900	888	888
8,900	8,950	893	893
8,950	9,000	898	898

9,000

At least	But less than	Single	Married filing jointly
9,000	9,050	903	903
9,050	9,100	908	908
9,100	9,150	913	913
9,150	9,200	918	918
9,200	9,250	923	923
9,250	9,300	930	928
9,300	9,350	938	933
9,350	9,400	945	938
9,400	9,450	953	943
9,450	9,500	960	948
9,500	9,550	968	953
9,550	9,600	975	958
9,600	9,650	983	963
9,650	9,700	990	968
9,700	9,750	998	973
9,750	9,800	1,005	978
9,800	9,850	1,013	983
9,850	9,900	1,020	988
9,900	9,950	1,028	993
9,950	10,000	1,035	998

10,000

At least	But less than	Single	Married filing jointly
10,000	10,050	1,043	1,003
10,050	10,100	1,050	1,008
10,100	10,150	1,058	1,013
10,150	10,200	1,065	1,018
10,200	10,250	1,073	1,023
10,250	10,300	1,080	1,028
10,300	10,350	1,088	1,033
10,350	10,400	1,095	1,038
10,400	10,450	1,103	1,043
10,450	10,500	1,110	1,048
10,500	10,550	1,118	1,053
10,550	10,600	1,125	1,058
10,600	10,650	1,133	1,063
10,650	10,700	1,140	1,068
10,700	10,750	1,148	1,073
10,750	10,800	1,155	1,078
10,800	10,850	1,163	1,083
10,850	10,900	1,170	1,088
10,900	10,950	1,178	1,093
10,950	11,000	1,185	1,098

11,000

At least	But less than	Single	Married filing jointly
11,000	11,050	1,193	1,103
11,050	11,100	1,200	1,108
11,100	11,150	1,208	1,113
11,150	11,200	1,215	1,118
11,200	11,250	1,223	1,123
11,250	11,300	1,230	1,128
11,300	11,350	1,238	1,133
11,350	11,400	1,245	1,138
11,400	11,450	1,253	1,143
11,450	11,500	1,260	1,148
11,500	11,550	1,268	1,153
11,550	11,600	1,275	1,158
11,600	11,650	1,283	1,163
11,650	11,700	1,290	1,168
11,700	11,750	1,298	1,173
11,750	11,800	1,305	1,178
11,800	11,850	1,313	1,183
11,850	11,900	1,320	1,188
11,900	11,950	1,328	1,193
11,950	12,000	1,335	1,198

12,000

At least	But less than	Single	Married filing jointly
12,000	12,050	1,343	1,203
12,050	12,100	1,350	1,208
12,100	12,150	1,358	1,213
12,150	12,200	1,365	1,218
12,200	12,250	1,373	1,223
12,250	12,300	1,380	1,228
12,300	12,350	1,388	1,233
12,350	12,400	1,395	1,238
12,400	12,450	1,403	1,243
12,450	12,500	1,410	1,248
12,500	12,550	1,418	1,253
12,550	12,600	1,425	1,258
12,600	12,650	1,433	1,263
12,650	12,700	1,440	1,268
12,700	12,750	1,448	1,273
12,750	12,800	1,455	1,278
12,800	12,850	1,463	1,283
12,850	12,900	1,470	1,288
12,900	12,950	1,478	1,293
12,950	13,000	1,485	1,298

13,000

At least	But less than	Single	Married filing jointly
13,000	13,050	1,493	1,303
13,050	13,100	1,500	1,308
13,100	13,150	1,508	1,313
13,150	13,200	1,515	1,318
13,200	13,250	1,523	1,323
13,250	13,300	1,530	1,328
13,300	13,350	1,538	1,333
13,350	13,400	1,545	1,338
13,400	13,450	1,553	1,343
13,450	13,500	1,560	1,348
13,500	13,550	1,568	1,353
13,550	13,600	1,575	1,358
13,600	13,650	1,583	1,363
13,650	13,700	1,590	1,368
13,700	13,750	1,598	1,373
13,750	13,800	1,605	1,378
13,800	13,850	1,613	1,383
13,850	13,900	1,620	1,388
13,900	13,950	1,628	1,393
13,950	14,000	1,635	1,398

14,000

At least	But less than	Single	Married filing jointly
14,000	14,050	1,643	1,403
14,050	14,100	1,650	1,408
14,100	14,150	1,658	1,413
14,150	14,200	1,665	1,418
14,200	14,250	1,673	1,423
14,250	14,300	1,680	1,428
14,300	14,350	1,688	1,433
14,350	14,400	1,695	1,438
14,400	14,450	1,703	1,443
14,450	14,500	1,710	1,448
14,500	14,550	1,718	1,453
14,550	14,600	1,725	1,458
14,600	14,650	1,733	1,463
14,650	14,700	1,740	1,468
14,700	14,750	1,748	1,473
14,750	14,800	1,755	1,478
14,800	14,850	1,763	1,483
14,850	14,900	1,770	1,488
14,900	14,950	1,778	1,493
14,950	15,000	1,785	1,498

15,000

At least	But less than	Single	Married filing jointly
15,000	15,050	1,793	1,503
15,050	15,100	1,800	1,508
15,100	15,150	1,808	1,513
15,150	15,200	1,815	1,518
15,200	15,250	1,823	1,523
15,250	15,300	1,830	1,528
15,300	15,350	1,838	1,533
15,350	15,400	1,845	1,538
15,400	15,450	1,853	1,543
15,450	15,500	1,860	1,548
15,500	15,550	1,868	1,553
15,550	15,600	1,875	1,558
15,600	15,650	1,883	1,563
15,650	15,700	1,890	1,568
15,700	15,750	1,898	1,573
15,750	15,800	1,905	1,578
15,800	15,850	1,913	1,583
15,850	15,900	1,920	1,588
15,900	15,950	1,928	1,593
15,950	16,000	1,935	1,598

16,000

At least	But less than	Single	Married filing jointly
16,000	16,050	1,943	1,603
16,050	16,100	1,950	1,608
16,100	16,150	1,958	1,613
16,150	16,200	1,965	1,618
16,200	16,250	1,973	1,623
16,250	16,300	1,980	1,628
16,300	16,350	1,988	1,633
16,350	16,400	1,995	1,638
16,400	16,450	2,003	1,643
16,450	16,500	2,010	1,648
16,500	16,550	2,018	1,653
16,550	16,600	2,025	1,658
16,600	16,650	2,033	1,663
16,650	16,700	2,040	1,668
16,700	16,750	2,048	1,673
16,750	16,800	2,055	1,678
16,800	16,850	2,063	1,683
16,850	16,900	2,070	1,688
16,900	16,950	2,078	1,693
16,950	17,000	2,085	1,698

(Continued)

17,000

At least	But less than	Single	Married filing jointly
17,000	17,050	2,093	1,703
17,050	17,100	2,100	1,708
17,100	17,150	2,108	1,713
17,150	17,200	2,115	1,718
17,200	17,250	2,123	1,723
17,250	17,300	2,130	1,728
17,300	17,350	2,138	1,733
17,350	17,400	2,145	1,738
17,400	17,450	2,153	1,743
17,450	17,500	2,160	1,748
17,500	17,550	2,168	1,753
17,550	17,600	2,175	1,758
17,600	17,650	2,183	1,763
17,650	17,700	2,190	1,768
17,700	17,750	2,198	1,773
17,750	17,800	2,205	1,778
17,800	17,850	2,213	1,783
17,850	17,900	2,220	1,788
17,900	17,950	2,228	1,793
17,950	18,000	2,235	1,798

18,000

At least	But less than	Single	Married filing jointly
18,000	18,050	2,243	1,803
18,050	18,100	2,250	1,808
18,100	18,150	2,258	1,813
18,150	18,200	2,265	1,818
18,200	18,250	2,273	1,823
18,250	18,300	2,280	1,828
18,300	18,350	2,288	1,833
18,350	18,400	2,295	1,838
18,400	18,450	2,303	1,843
18,450	18,500	2,310	1,849
18,500	18,550	2,318	1,856
18,550	18,600	2,325	1,864
18,600	18,650	2,333	1,871
18,650	18,700	2,340	1,879
18,700	18,750	2,348	1,886
18,750	18,800	2,355	1,894
18,800	18,850	2,363	1,901
18,850	18,900	2,370	1,909
18,900	18,950	2,378	1,916
18,950	19,000	2,385	1,924

19,000

At least	But less than	Single	Married filing jointly
19,000	19,050	2,393	1,931
19,050	19,100	2,400	1,939
19,100	19,150	2,408	1,946
19,150	19,200	2,415	1,954
19,200	19,250	2,423	1,961
19,250	19,300	2,430	1,969
19,300	19,350	2,438	1,976
19,350	19,400	2,445	1,984
19,400	19,450	2,453	1,991
19,450	19,500	2,460	1,999
19,500	19,550	2,468	2,006
19,550	19,600	2,475	2,014
19,600	19,650	2,483	2,021
19,650	19,700	2,490	2,029
19,700	19,750	2,498	2,036
19,750	19,800	2,505	2,044
19,800	19,850	2,513	2,051
19,850	19,900	2,520	2,059
19,900	19,950	2,528	2,066
19,950	20,000	2,535	2,074

20,000

At least	But less than	Single	Married filing jointly
20,000	20,050	2,543	2,081
20,050	20,100	2,550	2,089
20,100	20,150	2,558	2,096
20,150	20,200	2,565	2,104
20,200	20,250	2,573	2,111
20,250	20,300	2,580	2,119
20,300	20,350	2,588	2,126
20,350	20,400	2,595	2,134
20,400	20,450	2,603	2,141
20,450	20,500	2,610	2,149
20,500	20,550	2,618	2,156
20,550	20,600	2,625	2,164
20,600	20,650	2,633	2,171
20,650	20,700	2,640	2,179
20,700	20,750	2,648	2,186
20,750	20,800	2,655	2,194
20,800	20,850	2,663	2,201
20,850	20,900	2,670	2,209
20,900	20,950	2,678	2,216
20,950	21,000	2,685	2,224

21,000

At least	But less than	Single	Married filing jointly
21,000	21,050	2,693	2,231
21,050	21,100	2,700	2,239
21,100	21,150	2,708	2,246
21,150	21,200	2,715	2,254
21,200	21,250	2,723	2,261
21,250	21,300	2,730	2,269
21,300	21,350	2,738	2,276
21,350	21,400	2,745	2,284
21,400	21,450	2,753	2,291
21,450	21,500	2,760	2,299
21,500	21,550	2,768	2,306
21,550	21,600	2,775	2,314
21,600	21,650	2,783	2,321
21,650	21,700	2,790	2,329
21,700	21,750	2,798	2,336
21,750	21,800	2,805	2,344
21,800	21,850	2,813	2,351
21,850	21,900	2,820	2,359
21,900	21,950	2,828	2,366
21,950	22,000	2,835	2,374

22,000

At least	But less than	Single	Married filing jointly
22,000	22,050	2,843	2,381
22,050	22,100	2,850	2,389
22,100	22,150	2,858	2,396
22,150	22,200	2,865	2,404
22,200	22,250	2,873	2,411
22,250	22,300	2,880	2,419
22,300	22,350	2,888	2,426
22,350	22,400	2,895	2,434
22,400	22,450	2,903	2,441
22,450	22,500	2,910	2,449
22,500	22,550	2,918	2,456
22,550	22,600	2,925	2,464
22,600	22,650	2,933	2,471
22,650	22,700	2,940	2,479
22,700	22,750	2,948	2,486
22,750	22,800	2,955	2,494
22,800	22,850	2,963	2,501
22,850	22,900	2,970	2,509
22,900	22,950	2,978	2,516
22,950	23,000	2,985	2,524

23,000

At least	But less than	Single	Married filing jointly
23,000	23,050	2,993	2,531
23,050	23,100	3,000	2,539
23,100	23,150	3,008	2,546
23,150	23,200	3,015	2,554
23,200	23,250	3,023	2,561
23,250	23,300	3,030	2,569
23,300	23,350	3,038	2,576
23,350	23,400	3,045	2,584
23,400	23,450	3,053	2,591
23,450	23,500	3,060	2,599
23,500	23,550	3,068	2,606
23,550	23,600	3,075	2,614
23,600	23,650	3,083	2,621
23,650	23,700	3,090	2,629
23,700	23,750	3,098	2,636
23,750	23,800	3,105	2,644
23,800	23,850	3,113	2,651
23,850	23,900	3,120	2,659
23,900	23,950	3,128	2,666
23,950	24,000	3,135	2,674

24,000

At least	But less than	Single	Married filing jointly
24,000	24,050	3,143	2,681
24,050	24,100	3,150	2,689
24,100	24,150	3,158	2,696
24,150	24,200	3,165	2,704
24,200	24,250	3,173	2,711
24,250	24,300	3,180	2,719
24,300	24,350	3,188	2,726
24,350	24,400	3,195	2,734
24,400	24,450	3,203	2,741
24,450	24,500	3,210	2,749
24,500	24,550	3,218	2,756
24,550	24,600	3,225	2,764
24,600	24,650	3,233	2,771
24,650	24,700	3,240	2,779
24,700	24,750	3,248	2,786
24,750	24,800	3,255	2,794
24,800	24,850	3,263	2,801
24,850	24,900	3,270	2,809
24,900	24,950	3,278	2,816
24,950	25,000	3,285	2,824

25,000

At least	But less than	Single	Married filing jointly
25,000	25,050	3,293	2,831
25,050	25,100	3,300	2,839
25,100	25,150	3,308	2,846
25,150	25,200	3,315	2,854
25,200	25,250	3,323	2,861
25,250	25,300	3,330	2,869
25,300	25,350	3,338	2,876
25,350	25,400	3,345	2,884
25,400	25,450	3,353	2,891
25,450	25,500	3,360	2,899
25,500	25,550	3,368	2,906
25,550	25,600	3,375	2,914
25,600	25,650	3,383	2,921
25,650	25,700	3,390	2,929
25,700	25,750	3,398	2,936
25,750	25,800	3,405	2,944
25,800	25,850	3,413	2,951
25,850	25,900	3,420	2,959
25,900	25,950	3,428	2,966
25,950	26,000	3,435	2,974

26,000

At least	But less than	Single	Married filing jointly
26,000	26,050	3,443	2,981
26,050	26,100	3,450	2,989
26,100	26,150	3,458	2,996
26,150	26,200	3,465	3,004
26,200	26,250	3,473	3,011
26,250	26,300	3,480	3,019
26,300	26,350	3,488	3,026
26,350	26,400	3,495	3,034
26,400	26,450	3,503	3,041
26,450	26,500	3,510	3,049
26,500	26,550	3,518	3,056
26,550	26,600	3,525	3,064
26,600	26,650	3,533	3,071
26,650	26,700	3,540	3,079
26,700	26,750	3,548	3,086
26,750	26,800	3,555	3,094
26,800	26,850	3,563	3,101
26,850	26,900	3,570	3,109
26,900	26,950	3,578	3,116
26,950	27,000	3,585	3,124

27,000

At least	But less than	Single	Married filing jointly
27,000	27,050	3,593	3,131
27,050	27,100	3,600	3,139
27,100	27,150	3,608	3,146
27,150	27,200	3,615	3,154
27,200	27,250	3,623	3,161
27,250	27,300	3,630	3,169
27,300	27,350	3,638	3,176
27,350	27,400	3,645	3,184
27,400	27,450	3,653	3,191
27,450	27,500	3,660	3,199
27,500	27,550	3,668	3,206
27,550	27,600	3,675	3,214
27,600	27,650	3,683	3,221
27,650	27,700	3,690	3,229
27,700	27,750	3,698	3,236
27,750	27,800	3,705	3,244
27,800	27,850	3,713	3,251
27,850	27,900	3,720	3,259
27,900	27,950	3,728	3,266
27,950	28,000	3,735	3,274

28,000

At least	But less than	Single	Married filing jointly
28,000	28,050	3,743	3,281
28,050	28,100	3,750	3,289
28,100	28,150	3,758	3,296
28,150	28,200	3,765	3,304
28,200	28,250	3,773	3,311
28,250	28,300	3,780	3,319
28,300	28,350	3,788	3,326
28,350	28,400	3,795	3,334
28,400	28,450	3,803	3,341
28,450	28,500	3,810	3,349
28,500	28,550	3,818	3,356
28,550	28,600	3,825	3,364
28,600	28,650	3,833	3,371
28,650	28,700	3,840	3,379
28,700	28,750	3,848	3,386
28,750	28,800	3,855	3,394
28,800	28,850	3,863	3,401
28,850	28,900	3,870	3,409
28,900	28,950	3,878	3,416
28,950	29,000	3,885	3,424

(Continued)

Instructions for Form 1040EZ

If Form 1040EZ, line 6, is–		And you are–	
At least	But less than	Single	Married filing jointly
		Your tax is–	

29,000

At least	But less than	Single	Married filing jointly
29,000	29,050	3,893	3,431
29,050	29,100	3,900	3,439
29,100	29,150	3,908	3,446
29,150	29,200	3,915	3,454
29,200	29,250	3,923	3,461
29,250	29,300	3,930	3,469
29,300	29,350	3,938	3,476
29,350	29,400	3,945	3,484
29,400	29,450	3,953	3,491
29,450	29,500	3,960	3,499
29,500	29,550	3,968	3,506
29,550	29,600	3,975	3,514
29,600	29,650	3,983	3,521
29,650	29,700	3,990	3,529
29,700	29,750	3,998	3,536
29,750	29,800	4,005	3,544
29,800	29,850	4,013	3,551
29,850	29,900	4,020	3,559
29,900	29,950	4,028	3,566
29,950	30,000	4,035	3,574

30,000

At least	But less than	Single	Married filing jointly
30,000	30,050	4,043	3,581
30,050	30,100	4,050	3,589
30,100	30,150	4,058	3,596
30,150	30,200	4,065	3,604
30,200	30,250	4,073	3,611
30,250	30,300	4,080	3,619
30,300	30,350	4,088	3,626
30,350	30,400	4,095	3,634
30,400	30,450	4,103	3,641
30,450	30,500	4,110	3,649
30,500	30,550	4,118	3,656
30,550	30,600	4,125	3,664
30,600	30,650	4,133	3,671
30,650	30,700	4,140	3,679
30,700	30,750	4,148	3,686
30,750	30,800	4,155	3,694
30,800	30,850	4,163	3,701
30,850	30,900	4,170	3,709
30,900	30,950	4,178	3,716
30,950	31,000	4,185	3,724

31,000

At least	But less than	Single	Married filing jointly
31,000	31,050	4,193	3,731
31,050	31,100	4,200	3,739
31,100	31,150	4,208	3,746
31,150	31,200	4,215	3,754
31,200	31,250	4,223	3,761
31,250	31,300	4,230	3,769
31,300	31,350	4,238	3,776
31,350	31,400	4,245	3,784
31,400	31,450	4,253	3,791
31,450	31,500	4,260	3,799
31,500	31,550	4,268	3,806
31,550	31,600	4,275	3,814
31,600	31,650	4,283	3,821
31,650	31,700	4,290	3,829
31,700	31,750	4,298	3,836
31,750	31,800	4,305	3,844
31,800	31,850	4,313	3,851
31,850	31,900	4,320	3,859
31,900	31,950	4,328	3,866
31,950	32,000	4,335	3,874

32,000

At least	But less than	Single	Married filing jointly
32,000	32,050	4,343	3,881
32,050	32,100	4,350	3,889
32,100	32,150	4,358	3,896
32,150	32,200	4,365	3,904
32,200	32,250	4,373	3,911
32,250	32,300	4,380	3,919
32,300	32,350	4,388	3,926
32,350	32,400	4,395	3,934
32,400	32,450	4,403	3,941
32,450	32,500	4,410	3,949
32,500	32,550	4,418	3,956
32,550	32,600	4,425	3,964
32,600	32,650	4,433	3,971
32,650	32,700	4,440	3,979
32,700	32,750	4,448	3,986
32,750	32,800	4,455	3,994
32,800	32,850	4,463	4,001
32,850	32,900	4,470	4,009
32,900	32,950	4,478	4,016
32,950	33,000	4,485	4,024

33,000

At least	But less than	Single	Married filing jointly
33,000	33,050	4,493	4,031
33,050	33,100	4,500	4,039
33,100	33,150	4,508	4,046
33,150	33,200	4,515	4,054
33,200	33,250	4,523	4,061
33,250	33,300	4,530	4,069
33,300	33,350	4,538	4,076
33,350	33,400	4,545	4,084
33,400	33,450	4,553	4,091
33,450	33,500	4,560	4,099
33,500	33,550	4,568	4,106
33,550	33,600	4,575	4,114
33,600	33,650	4,583	4,121
33,650	33,700	4,590	4,129
33,700	33,750	4,598	4,136
33,750	33,800	4,605	4,144
33,800	33,850	4,613	4,151
33,850	33,900	4,620	4,159
33,900	33,950	4,628	4,166
33,950	34,000	4,635	4,174

34,000

At least	But less than	Single	Married filing jointly
34,000	34,050	4,643	4,181
34,050	34,100	4,650	4,189
34,100	34,150	4,658	4,196
34,150	34,200	4,665	4,204
34,200	34,250	4,673	4,211
34,250	34,300	4,680	4,219
34,300	34,350	4,688	4,226
34,350	34,400	4,695	4,234
34,400	34,450	4,703	4,241
34,450	34,500	4,710	4,249
34,500	34,550	4,718	4,256
34,550	34,600	4,725	4,264
34,600	34,650	4,733	4,271
34,650	34,700	4,740	4,279
34,700	34,750	4,748	4,286
34,750	34,800	4,755	4,294
34,800	34,850	4,763	4,301
34,850	34,900	4,770	4,309
34,900	34,950	4,778	4,316
34,950	35,000	4,785	4,324

35,000

At least	But less than	Single	Married filing jointly
35,000	35,050	4,793	4,331
35,050	35,100	4,800	4,339
35,100	35,150	4,808	4,346
35,150	35,200	4,815	4,354
35,200	35,250	4,823	4,361
35,250	35,300	4,830	4,369
35,300	35,350	4,838	4,376
35,350	35,400	4,845	4,384
35,400	35,450	4,853	4,391
35,450	35,500	4,860	4,399
35,500	35,550	4,868	4,406
35,550	35,600	4,875	4,414
35,600	35,650	4,883	4,421
35,650	35,700	4,890	4,429
35,700	35,750	4,898	4,436
35,750	35,800	4,905	4,444
35,800	35,850	4,913	4,451
35,850	35,900	4,920	4,459
35,900	35,950	4,928	4,466
35,950	36,000	4,935	4,474

36,000

At least	But less than	Single	Married filing jointly
36,000	36,050	4,943	4,481
36,050	36,100	4,950	4,489
36,100	36,150	4,958	4,496
36,150	36,200	4,965	4,504
36,200	36,250	4,973	4,511
36,250	36,300	4,980	4,519
36,300	36,350	4,988	4,526
36,350	36,400	4,995	4,534
36,400	36,450	5,003	4,541
36,450	36,500	5,010	4,549
36,500	36,550	5,018	4,556
36,550	36,600	5,025	4,564
36,600	36,650	5,033	4,571
36,650	36,700	5,040	4,579
36,700	36,750	5,048	4,586
36,750	36,800	5,055	4,594
36,800	36,850	5,063	4,601
36,850	36,900	5,070	4,609
36,900	36,950	5,078	4,616
36,950	37,000	5,085	4,624

37,000

At least	But less than	Single	Married filing jointly
37,000	37,050	5,093	4,631
37,050	37,100	5,100	4,639
37,100	37,150	5,108	4,646
37,150	37,200	5,115	4,654
37,200	37,250	5,123	4,661
37,250	37,300	5,130	4,669
37,300	37,350	5,138	4,676
37,350	37,400	5,145	4,684
37,400	37,450	5,153	4,691
37,450	37,500	5,163	4,699
37,500	37,550	5,175	4,706
37,550	37,600	5,188	4,714
37,600	37,650	5,200	4,721
37,650	37,700	5,213	4,729
37,700	37,750	5,225	4,736
37,750	37,800	5,238	4,744
37,800	37,850	5,250	4,751
37,850	37,900	5,263	4,759
37,900	37,950	5,275	4,766
37,950	38,000	5,288	4,774

38,000

At least	But less than	Single	Married filing jointly
38,000	38,050	5,300	4,781
38,050	38,100	5,313	4,789
38,100	38,150	5,325	4,796
38,150	38,200	5,338	4,804
38,200	38,250	5,350	4,811
38,250	38,300	5,363	4,819
38,300	38,350	5,375	4,826
38,350	38,400	5,388	4,834
38,400	38,450	5,400	4,841
38,450	38,500	5,413	4,849
38,500	38,550	5,425	4,856
38,550	38,600	5,438	4,864
38,600	38,650	5,450	4,871
38,650	38,700	5,463	4,879
38,700	38,750	5,475	4,886
38,750	38,800	5,488	4,894
38,800	38,850	5,500	4,901
38,850	38,900	5,513	4,909
38,900	38,950	5,525	4,916
38,950	39,000	5,538	4,924

39,000

At least	But less than	Single	Married filing jointly
39,000	39,050	5,550	4,931
39,050	39,100	5,563	4,939
39,100	39,150	5,575	4,946
39,150	39,200	5,588	4,954
39,200	39,250	5,600	4,961
39,250	39,300	5,613	4,969
39,300	39,350	5,625	4,976
39,350	39,400	5,638	4,984
39,400	39,450	5,650	4,991
39,450	39,500	5,663	4,999
39,500	39,550	5,675	5,006
39,550	39,600	5,688	5,014
39,600	39,650	5,700	5,021
39,650	39,700	5,713	5,029
39,700	39,750	5,725	5,036
39,750	39,800	5,738	5,044
39,800	39,850	5,750	5,051
39,850	39,900	5,763	5,059
39,900	39,950	5,775	5,066
39,950	40,000	5,788	5,074

40,000

At least	But less than	Single	Married filing jointly
40,000	40,050	5,800	5,081
40,050	40,100	5,813	5,089
40,100	40,150	5,825	5,096
40,150	40,200	5,838	5,104
40,200	40,250	5,850	5,111
40,250	40,300	5,863	5,119
40,300	40,350	5,875	5,126
40,350	40,400	5,888	5,134
40,400	40,450	5,900	5,141
40,450	40,500	5,913	5,149
40,500	40,550	5,925	5,156
40,550	40,600	5,938	5,164
40,600	40,650	5,950	5,171
40,650	40,700	5,963	5,179
40,700	40,750	5,975	5,186
40,750	40,800	5,988	5,194
40,800	40,850	6,000	5,201
40,850	40,900	6,013	5,209
40,900	40,950	6,025	5,216
40,950	41,000	6,038	5,224

(Continued)

| If Form 1040EZ, line 6, is– | | And you are– | |
At least	But less than	Single	Married filing jointly
		Your tax is–	

41,000

At least	But less than	Single	Married filing jointly
41,000	41,050	6,050	5,231
41,050	41,100	6,063	5,239
41,100	41,150	6,075	5,246
41,150	41,200	6,088	5,254
41,200	41,250	6,100	5,261
41,250	41,300	6,113	5,269
41,300	41,350	6,125	5,276
41,350	41,400	6,138	5,284
41,400	41,450	6,150	5,291
41,450	41,500	6,163	5,299
41,500	41,550	6,175	5,306
41,550	41,600	6,188	5,314
41,600	41,650	6,200	5,321
41,650	41,700	6,213	5,329
41,700	41,750	6,225	5,336
41,750	41,800	6,238	5,344
41,800	41,850	6,250	5,351
41,850	41,900	6,263	5,359
41,900	41,950	6,275	5,366
41,950	42,000	6,288	5,374

42,000

At least	But less than	Single	Married filing jointly
42,000	42,050	6,300	5,381
42,050	42,100	6,313	5,389
42,100	42,150	6,325	5,396
42,150	42,200	6,338	5,404
42,200	42,250	6,350	5,411
42,250	42,300	6,363	5,419
42,300	42,350	6,375	5,426
42,350	42,400	6,388	5,434
42,400	42,450	6,400	5,441
42,450	42,500	6,413	5,449
42,500	42,550	6,425	5,456
42,550	42,600	6,438	5,464
42,600	42,650	6,450	5,471
42,650	42,700	6,463	5,479
42,700	42,750	6,475	5,486
42,750	42,800	6,488	5,494
42,800	42,850	6,500	5,501
42,850	42,900	6,513	5,509
42,900	42,950	6,525	5,516
42,950	43,000	6,538	5,524

43,000

At least	But less than	Single	Married filing jointly
43,000	43,050	6,550	5,531
43,050	43,100	6,563	5,539
43,100	43,150	6,575	5,546
43,150	43,200	6,588	5,554
43,200	43,250	6,600	5,561
43,250	43,300	6,613	5,569
43,300	43,350	6,625	5,576
43,350	43,400	6,638	5,584
43,400	43,450	6,650	5,591
43,450	43,500	6,663	5,599
43,500	43,550	6,675	5,606
43,550	43,600	6,688	5,614
43,600	43,650	6,700	5,621
43,650	43,700	6,713	5,629
43,700	43,750	6,725	5,636
43,750	43,800	6,738	5,644
43,800	43,850	6,750	5,651
43,850	43,900	6,763	5,659
43,900	43,950	6,775	5,666
43,950	44,000	6,788	5,674

44,000

At least	But less than	Single	Married filing jointly
44,000	44,050	6,800	5,681
44,050	44,100	6,813	5,689
44,100	44,150	6,825	5,696
44,150	44,200	6,838	5,704
44,200	44,250	6,850	5,711
44,250	44,300	6,863	5,719
44,300	44,350	6,875	5,726
44,350	44,400	6,888	5,734
44,400	44,450	6,900	5,741
44,450	44,500	6,913	5,749
44,500	44,550	6,925	5,756
44,550	44,600	6,938	5,764
44,600	44,650	6,950	5,771
44,650	44,700	6,963	5,779
44,700	44,750	6,975	5,786
44,750	44,800	6,988	5,794
44,800	44,850	7,000	5,801
44,850	44,900	7,013	5,809
44,900	44,950	7,025	5,816
44,950	45,000	7,038	5,824

45,000

At least	But less than	Single	Married filing jointly
45,000	45,050	7,050	5,831
45,050	45,100	7,063	5,839
45,100	45,150	7,075	5,846
45,150	45,200	7,088	5,854
45,200	45,250	7,100	5,861
45,250	45,300	7,113	5,869
45,300	45,350	7,125	5,876
45,350	45,400	7,138	5,884
45,400	45,450	7,150	5,891
45,450	45,500	7,163	5,899
45,500	45,550	7,175	5,906
45,550	45,600	7,188	5,914
45,600	45,650	7,200	5,921
45,650	45,700	7,213	5,929
45,700	45,750	7,225	5,936
45,750	45,800	7,238	5,944
45,800	45,850	7,250	5,951
45,850	45,900	7,263	5,959
45,900	45,950	7,275	5,966
45,950	46,000	7,288	5,974

46,000

At least	But less than	Single	Married filing jointly
46,000	46,050	7,300	5,981
46,050	46,100	7,313	5,989
46,100	46,150	7,325	5,996
46,150	46,200	7,338	6,004
46,200	46,250	7,350	6,011
46,250	46,300	7,363	6,019
46,300	46,350	7,375	6,026
46,350	46,400	7,388	6,034
46,400	46,450	7,400	6,041
46,450	46,500	7,413	6,049
46,500	46,550	7,425	6,056
46,550	46,600	7,438	6,064
46,600	46,650	7,450	6,071
46,650	46,700	7,463	6,079
46,700	46,750	7,475	6,086
46,750	46,800	7,488	6,094
46,800	46,850	7,500	6,101
46,850	46,900	7,513	6,109
46,900	46,950	7,525	6,116
46,950	47,000	7,538	6,124

47,000

At least	But less than	Single	Married filing jointly
47,000	47,050	7,550	6,131
47,050	47,100	7,563	6,139
47,100	47,150	7,575	6,146
47,150	47,200	7,588	6,154
47,200	47,250	7,600	6,161
47,250	47,300	7,613	6,169
47,300	47,350	7,625	6,176
47,350	47,400	7,638	6,184
47,400	47,450	7,650	6,191
47,450	47,500	7,663	6,199
47,500	47,550	7,675	6,206
47,550	47,600	7,688	6,214
47,600	47,650	7,700	6,221
47,650	47,700	7,713	6,229
47,700	47,750	7,725	6,236
47,750	47,800	7,738	6,244
47,800	47,850	7,750	6,251
47,850	47,900	7,763	6,259
47,900	47,950	7,775	6,266
47,950	48,000	7,788	6,274

48,000

At least	But less than	Single	Married filing jointly
48,000	48,050	7,800	6,281
48,050	48,100	7,813	6,289
48,100	48,150	7,825	6,296
48,150	48,200	7,838	6,304
48,200	48,250	7,850	6,311
48,250	48,300	7,863	6,319
48,300	48,350	7,875	6,326
48,350	48,400	7,888	6,334
48,400	48,450	7,900	6,341
48,450	48,500	7,913	6,349
48,500	48,550	7,925	6,356
48,550	48,600	7,938	6,364
48,600	48,650	7,950	6,371
48,650	48,700	7,963	6,379
48,700	48,750	7,975	6,386
48,750	48,800	7,988	6,394
48,800	48,850	8,000	6,401
48,850	48,900	8,013	6,409
48,900	48,950	8,025	6,416
48,950	49,000	8,038	6,424

49,000

At least	But less than	Single	Married filing jointly
49,000	49,050	8,050	6,431
49,050	49,100	8,063	6,439
49,100	49,150	8,075	6,446
49,150	49,200	8,088	6,454
49,200	49,250	8,100	6,461
49,250	49,300	8,113	6,469
49,300	49,350	8,125	6,476
49,350	49,400	8,138	6,484
49,400	49,450	8,150	6,491
49,450	49,500	8,163	6,499
49,500	49,550	8,175	6,506
49,550	49,600	8,188	6,514
49,600	49,650	8,200	6,521
49,650	49,700	8,213	6,529
49,700	49,750	8,225	6,536
49,750	49,800	8,238	6,544
49,800	49,850	8,250	6,551
49,850	49,900	8,263	6,559
49,900	49,950	8,275	6,566
49,950	50,000	8,288	6,574

50,000

At least	But less than	Single	Married filing jointly
50,000	50,050	8,300	6,581
50,050	50,100	8,313	6,589
50,100	50,150	8,325	6,596
50,150	50,200	8,338	6,604
50,200	50,250	8,350	6,611
50,250	50,300	8,363	6,619
50,300	50,350	8,375	6,626
50,350	50,400	8,388	6,634
50,400	50,450	8,400	6,641
50,450	50,500	8,413	6,649
50,500	50,550	8,425	6,656
50,550	50,600	8,438	6,664
50,600	50,650	8,450	6,671
50,650	50,700	8,463	6,679
50,700	50,750	8,475	6,686
50,750	50,800	8,488	6,694
50,800	50,850	8,500	6,701
50,850	50,900	8,513	6,709
50,900	50,950	8,525	6,716
50,950	51,000	8,538	6,724

51,000

At least	But less than	Single	Married filing jointly
51,000	51,050	8,550	6,731
51,050	51,100	8,563	6,739
51,100	51,150	8,575	6,746
51,150	51,200	8,588	6,754
51,200	51,250	8,600	6,761
51,250	51,300	8,613	6,769
51,300	51,350	8,625	6,776
51,350	51,400	8,638	6,784
51,400	51,450	8,650	6,791
51,450	51,500	8,663	6,799
51,500	51,550	8,675	6,806
51,550	51,600	8,688	6,814
51,600	51,650	8,700	6,821
51,650	51,700	8,713	6,829
51,700	51,750	8,725	6,836
51,750	51,800	8,738	6,844
51,800	51,850	8,750	6,851
51,850	51,900	8,763	6,859
51,900	51,950	8,775	6,866
51,950	52,000	8,788	6,874

52,000

At least	But less than	Single	Married filing jointly
52,000	52,050	8,800	6,881
52,050	52,100	8,813	6,889
52,100	52,150	8,825	6,896
52,150	52,200	8,838	6,904
52,200	52,250	8,850	6,911
52,250	52,300	8,863	6,919
52,300	52,350	8,875	6,926
52,350	52,400	8,888	6,934
52,400	52,450	8,900	6,941
52,450	52,500	8,913	6,949
52,500	52,550	8,925	6,956
52,550	52,600	8,938	6,964
52,600	52,650	8,950	6,971
52,650	52,700	8,963	6,979
52,700	52,750	8,975	6,986
52,750	52,800	8,988	6,994
52,800	52,850	9,000	7,001
52,850	52,900	9,013	7,009
52,900	52,950	9,025	7,016
52,950	53,000	9,038	7,024

(Continued)

Instructions for Form 1040EZ

If Form 1040EZ, line 6, is–		And you are–	
At least	But less than	Single	Married filing jointly
		Your tax is–	

53,000

At least	But less than	Single	Married filing jointly
53,000	53,050	9,050	7,031
53,050	53,100	9,063	7,039
53,100	53,150	9,075	7,046
53,150	53,200	9,088	7,054
53,200	53,250	9,100	7,061
53,250	53,300	9,113	7,069
53,300	53,350	9,125	7,076
53,350	53,400	9,138	7,084
53,400	53,450	9,150	7,091
53,450	53,500	9,163	7,099
53,500	53,550	9,175	7,106
53,550	53,600	9,188	7,114
53,600	53,650	9,200	7,121
53,650	53,700	9,213	7,129
53,700	53,750	9,225	7,136
53,750	53,800	9,238	7,144
53,800	53,850	9,250	7,151
53,850	53,900	9,263	7,159
53,900	53,950	9,275	7,166
53,950	54,000	9,288	7,174

54,000

At least	But less than	Single	Married filing jointly
54,000	54,050	9,300	7,181
54,050	54,100	9,313	7,189
54,100	54,150	9,325	7,196
54,150	54,200	9,338	7,204
54,200	54,250	9,350	7,211
54,250	54,300	9,363	7,219
54,300	54,350	9,375	7,226
54,350	54,400	9,388	7,234
54,400	54,450	9,400	7,241
54,450	54,500	9,413	7,249
54,500	54,550	9,425	7,256
54,550	54,600	9,438	7,264
54,600	54,650	9,450	7,271
54,650	54,700	9,463	7,279
54,700	54,750	9,475	7,286
54,750	54,800	9,488	7,294
54,800	54,850	9,500	7,301
54,850	54,900	9,513	7,309
54,900	54,950	9,525	7,316
54,950	55,000	9,538	7,324

55,000

At least	But less than	Single	Married filing jointly
55,000	55,050	9,550	7,331
55,050	55,100	9,563	7,339
55,100	55,150	9,575	7,346
55,150	55,200	9,588	7,354
55,200	55,250	9,600	7,361
55,250	55,300	9,613	7,369
55,300	55,350	9,625	7,376
55,350	55,400	9,638	7,384
55,400	55,450	9,650	7,391
55,450	55,500	9,663	7,399
55,500	55,550	9,675	7,406
55,550	55,600	9,688	7,414
55,600	55,650	9,700	7,421
55,650	55,700	9,713	7,429
55,700	55,750	9,725	7,436
55,750	55,800	9,738	7,444
55,800	55,850	9,750	7,451
55,850	55,900	9,763	7,459
55,900	55,950	9,775	7,466
55,950	56,000	9,788	7,474

56,000

At least	But less than	Single	Married filing jointly
56,000	56,050	9,800	7,481
56,050	56,100	9,813	7,489
56,100	56,150	9,825	7,496
56,150	56,200	9,838	7,504
56,200	56,250	9,850	7,511
56,250	56,300	9,863	7,519
56,300	56,350	9,875	7,526
56,350	56,400	9,888	7,534
56,400	56,450	9,900	7,541
56,450	56,500	9,913	7,549
56,500	56,550	9,925	7,556
56,550	56,600	9,938	7,564
56,600	56,650	9,950	7,571
56,650	56,700	9,963	7,579
56,700	56,750	9,975	7,586
56,750	56,800	9,988	7,594
56,800	56,850	10,000	7,601
56,850	56,900	10,013	7,609
56,900	56,950	10,025	7,616
56,950	57,000	10,038	7,624

57,000

At least	But less than	Single	Married filing jointly
57,000	57,050	10,050	7,631
57,050	57,100	10,063	7,639
57,100	57,150	10,075	7,646
57,150	57,200	10,088	7,654
57,200	57,250	10,100	7,661
57,250	57,300	10,113	7,669
57,300	57,350	10,125	7,676
57,350	57,400	10,138	7,684
57,400	57,450	10,150	7,691
57,450	57,500	10,163	7,699
57,500	57,550	10,175	7,706
57,550	57,600	10,188	7,714
57,600	57,650	10,200	7,721
57,650	57,700	10,213	7,729
57,700	57,750	10,225	7,736
57,750	57,800	10,238	7,744
57,800	57,850	10,250	7,751
57,850	57,900	10,263	7,759
57,900	57,950	10,275	7,766
57,950	58,000	10,288	7,774

58,000

At least	But less than	Single	Married filing jointly
58,000	58,050	10,300	7,781
58,050	58,100	10,313	7,789
58,100	58,150	10,325	7,796
58,150	58,200	10,338	7,804
58,200	58,250	10,350	7,811
58,250	58,300	10,363	7,819
58,300	58,350	10,375	7,826
58,350	58,400	10,388	7,834
58,400	58,450	10,400	7,841
58,450	58,500	10,413	7,849
58,500	58,550	10,425	7,856
58,550	58,600	10,438	7,864
58,600	58,650	10,450	7,871
58,650	58,700	10,463	7,879
58,700	58,750	10,475	7,886
58,750	58,800	10,488	7,894
58,800	58,850	10,500	7,901
58,850	58,900	10,513	7,909
58,900	58,950	10,525	7,916
58,950	59,000	10,538	7,924

59,000

At least	But less than	Single	Married filing jointly
59,000	59,050	10,550	7,931
59,050	59,100	10,563	7,939
59,100	59,150	10,575	7,946
59,150	59,200	10,588	7,954
59,200	59,250	10,600	7,961
59,250	59,300	10,613	7,969
59,300	59,350	10,625	7,976
59,350	59,400	10,638	7,984
59,400	59,450	10,650	7,991
59,450	59,500	10,663	7,999
59,500	59,550	10,675	8,006
59,550	59,600	10,688	8,014
59,600	59,650	10,700	8,021
59,650	59,700	10,713	8,029
59,700	59,750	10,725	8,036
59,750	59,800	10,738	8,044
59,800	59,850	10,750	8,051
59,850	59,900	10,763	8,059
59,900	59,950	10,775	8,066
59,950	60,000	10,788	8,074

60,000

At least	But less than	Single	Married filing jointly
60,000	60,050	10,800	8,081
60,050	60,100	10,813	8,089
60,100	60,150	10,825	8,096
60,150	60,200	10,838	8,104
60,200	60,250	10,850	8,111
60,250	60,300	10,863	8,119
60,300	60,350	10,875	8,126
60,350	60,400	10,888	8,134
60,400	60,450	10,900	8,141
60,450	60,500	10,913	8,149
60,500	60,550	10,925	8,156
60,550	60,600	10,938	8,164
60,600	60,650	10,950	8,171
60,650	60,700	10,963	8,179
60,700	60,750	10,975	8,186
60,750	60,800	10,988	8,194
60,800	60,850	11,000	8,201
60,850	60,900	11,013	8,209
60,900	60,950	11,025	8,216
60,950	61,000	11,038	8,224

61,000

At least	But less than	Single	Married filing jointly
61,000	61,050	11,050	8,231
61,050	61,100	11,063	8,239
61,100	61,150	11,075	8,246
61,150	61,200	11,088	8,254
61,200	61,250	11,100	8,261
61,250	61,300	11,113	8,269
61,300	61,350	11,125	8,276
61,350	61,400	11,138	8,284
61,400	61,450	11,150	8,291
61,450	61,500	11,163	8,299
61,500	61,550	11,175	8,306
61,550	61,600	11,188	8,314
61,600	61,650	11,200	8,321
61,650	61,700	11,213	8,329
61,700	61,750	11,225	8,336
61,750	61,800	11,238	8,344
61,800	61,850	11,250	8,351
61,850	61,900	11,263	8,359
61,900	61,950	11,275	8,366
61,950	62,000	11,288	8,374

62,000

At least	But less than	Single	Married filing jointly
62,000	62,050	11,300	8,381
62,050	62,100	11,313	8,389
62,100	62,150	11,325	8,396
62,150	62,200	11,338	8,404
62,200	62,250	11,350	8,411
62,250	62,300	11,363	8,419
62,300	62,350	11,375	8,426
62,350	62,400	11,388	8,434
62,400	62,450	11,400	8,441
62,450	62,500	11,413	8,449
62,500	62,550	11,425	8,456
62,550	62,600	11,438	8,464
62,600	62,650	11,450	8,471
62,650	62,700	11,463	8,479
62,700	62,750	11,475	8,486
62,750	62,800	11,488	8,494
62,800	62,850	11,500	8,501
62,850	62,900	11,513	8,509
62,900	62,950	11,525	8,516
62,950	63,000	11,538	8,524

63,000

At least	But less than	Single	Married filing jointly
63,000	63,050	11,550	8,531
63,050	63,100	11,563	8,539
63,100	63,150	11,575	8,546
63,150	63,200	11,588	8,554
63,200	63,250	11,600	8,561
63,250	63,300	11,613	8,569
63,300	63,350	11,625	8,576
63,350	63,400	11,638	8,584
63,400	63,450	11,650	8,591
63,450	63,500	11,663	8,599
63,500	63,550	11,675	8,606
63,550	63,600	11,688	8,614
63,600	63,650	11,700	8,621
63,650	63,700	11,713	8,629
63,700	63,750	11,725	8,636
63,750	63,800	11,738	8,644
63,800	63,850	11,750	8,651
63,850	63,900	11,763	8,659
63,900	63,950	11,775	8,666
63,950	64,000	11,788	8,674

64,000

At least	But less than	Single	Married filing jointly
64,000	64,050	11,800	8,681
64,050	64,100	11,813	8,689
64,100	64,150	11,825	8,696
64,150	64,200	11,838	8,704
64,200	64,250	11,850	8,711
64,250	64,300	11,863	8,719
64,300	64,350	11,875	8,726
64,350	64,400	11,888	8,734
64,400	64,450	11,900	8,741
64,450	64,500	11,913	8,749
64,500	64,550	11,925	8,756
64,550	64,600	11,938	8,764
64,600	64,650	11,950	8,771
64,650	64,700	11,963	8,779
64,700	64,750	11,975	8,786
64,750	64,800	11,988	8,794
64,800	64,850	12,000	8,801
64,850	64,900	12,013	8,809
64,900	64,950	12,025	8,816
64,950	65,000	12,038	8,824

(Continued)

65,000

At least	But less than	Single	Married filing jointly
65,000	65,050	12,050	8,831
65,050	65,100	12,063	8,839
65,100	65,150	12,075	8,846
65,150	65,200	12,088	8,854
65,200	65,250	12,100	8,861
65,250	65,300	12,113	8,869
65,300	65,350	12,125	8,876
65,350	65,400	12,138	8,884
65,400	65,450	12,150	8,891
65,450	65,500	12,163	8,899
65,500	65,550	12,175	8,906
65,550	65,600	12,188	8,914
65,600	65,650	12,200	8,921
65,650	65,700	12,213	8,929
65,700	65,750	12,225	8,936
65,750	65,800	12,238	8,944
65,800	65,850	12,250	8,951
65,850	65,900	12,263	8,959
65,900	65,950	12,275	8,966
65,950	66,000	12,288	8,974

66,000

At least	But less than	Single	Married filing jointly
66,000	66,050	12,300	8,981
66,050	66,100	12,313	8,989
66,100	66,150	12,325	8,996
66,150	66,200	12,338	9,004
66,200	66,250	12,350	9,011
66,250	66,300	12,363	9,019
66,300	66,350	12,375	9,026
66,350	66,400	12,388	9,034
66,400	66,450	12,400	9,041
66,450	66,500	12,413	9,049
66,500	66,550	12,425	9,056
66,550	66,600	12,438	9,064
66,600	66,650	12,450	9,071
66,650	66,700	12,463	9,079
66,700	66,750	12,475	9,086
66,750	66,800	12,488	9,094
66,800	66,850	12,500	9,101
66,850	66,900	12,513	9,109
66,900	66,950	12,525	9,116
66,950	67,000	12,538	9,124

67,000

At least	But less than	Single	Married filing jointly
67,000	67,050	12,550	9,131
67,050	67,100	12,563	9,139
67,100	67,150	12,575	9,146
67,150	67,200	12,588	9,154
67,200	67,250	12,600	9,161
67,250	67,300	12,613	9,169
67,300	67,350	12,625	9,176
67,350	67,400	12,638	9,184
67,400	67,450	12,650	9,191
67,450	67,500	12,663	9,199
67,500	67,550	12,675	9,206
67,550	67,600	12,688	9,214
67,600	67,650	12,700	9,221
67,650	67,700	12,713	9,229
67,700	67,750	12,725	9,236
67,750	67,800	12,738	9,244
67,800	67,850	12,750	9,251
67,850	67,900	12,763	9,259
67,900	67,950	12,775	9,266
67,950	68,000	12,788	9,274

68,000

At least	But less than	Single	Married filing jointly
68,000	68,050	12,800	9,281
68,050	68,100	12,813	9,289
68,100	68,150	12,825	9,296
68,150	68,200	12,838	9,304
68,200	68,250	12,850	9,311
68,250	68,300	12,863	9,319
68,300	68,350	12,875	9,326
68,350	68,400	12,888	9,334
68,400	68,450	12,900	9,341
68,450	68,500	12,913	9,349
68,500	68,550	12,925	9,356
68,550	68,600	12,938	9,364
68,600	68,650	12,950	9,371
68,650	68,700	12,963	9,379
68,700	68,750	12,975	9,386
68,750	68,800	12,988	9,394
68,800	68,850	13,000	9,401
68,850	68,900	13,013	9,409
68,900	68,950	13,025	9,416
68,950	69,000	13,038	9,424

69,000

At least	But less than	Single	Married filing jointly
69,000	69,050	13,050	9,431
69,050	69,100	13,063	9,439
69,100	69,150	13,075	9,446
69,150	69,200	13,088	9,454
69,200	69,250	13,100	9,461
69,250	69,300	13,113	9,469
69,300	69,350	13,125	9,476
69,350	69,400	13,138	9,484
69,400	69,450	13,150	9,491
69,450	69,500	13,163	9,499
69,500	69,550	13,175	9,506
69,550	69,600	13,188	9,514
69,600	69,650	13,200	9,521
69,650	69,700	13,213	9,529
69,700	69,750	13,225	9,536
69,750	69,800	13,238	9,544
69,800	69,850	13,250	9,551
69,850	69,900	13,263	9,559
69,900	69,950	13,275	9,566
69,950	70,000	13,288	9,574

70,000

At least	But less than	Single	Married filing jointly
70,000	70,050	13,300	9,581
70,050	70,100	13,313	9,589
70,100	70,150	13,325	9,596
70,150	70,200	13,338	9,604
70,200	70,250	13,350	9,611
70,250	70,300	13,363	9,619
70,300	70,350	13,375	9,626
70,350	70,400	13,388	9,634
70,400	70,450	13,400	9,641
70,450	70,500	13,413	9,649
70,500	70,550	13,425	9,656
70,550	70,600	13,438	9,664
70,600	70,650	13,450	9,671
70,650	70,700	13,463	9,679
70,700	70,750	13,475	9,686
70,750	70,800	13,488	9,694
70,800	70,850	13,500	9,701
70,850	70,900	13,513	9,709
70,900	70,950	13,525	9,716
70,950	71,000	13,538	9,724

71,000

At least	But less than	Single	Married filing jointly
71,000	71,050	13,550	9,731
71,050	71,100	13,563	9,739
71,100	71,150	13,575	9,746
71,150	71,200	13,588	9,754
71,200	71,250	13,600	9,761
71,250	71,300	13,613	9,769
71,300	71,350	13,625	9,776
71,350	71,400	13,638	9,784
71,400	71,450	13,650	9,791
71,450	71,500	13,663	9,799
71,500	71,550	13,675	9,806
71,550	71,600	13,688	9,814
71,600	71,650	13,700	9,821
71,650	71,700	13,713	9,829
71,700	71,750	13,725	9,836
71,750	71,800	13,738	9,844
71,800	71,850	13,750	9,851
71,850	71,900	13,763	9,859
71,900	71,950	13,775	9,866
71,950	72,000	13,788	9,874

72,000

At least	But less than	Single	Married filing jointly
72,000	72,050	13,800	9,881
72,050	72,100	13,813	9,889
72,100	72,150	13,825	9,896
72,150	72,200	13,838	9,904
72,200	72,250	13,850	9,911
72,250	72,300	13,863	9,919
72,300	72,350	13,875	9,926
72,350	72,400	13,888	9,934
72,400	72,450	13,900	9,941
72,450	72,500	13,913	9,949
72,500	72,550	13,925	9,956
72,550	72,600	13,938	9,964
72,600	72,650	13,950	9,971
72,650	72,700	13,963	9,979
72,700	72,750	13,975	9,986
72,750	72,800	13,988	9,994
72,800	72,850	14,000	10,001
72,850	72,900	14,013	10,009
72,900	72,950	14,025	10,016
72,950	73,000	14,038	10,024

73,000

At least	But less than	Single	Married filing jointly
73,000	73,050	14,050	10,031
73,050	73,100	14,063	10,039
73,100	73,150	14,075	10,046
73,150	73,200	14,088	10,054
73,200	73,250	14,100	10,061
73,250	73,300	14,113	10,069
73,300	73,350	14,125	10,076
73,350	73,400	14,138	10,084
73,400	73,450	14,150	10,091
73,450	73,500	14,163	10,099
73,500	73,550	14,175	10,106
73,550	73,600	14,188	10,114
73,600	73,650	14,200	10,121
73,650	73,700	14,213	10,129
73,700	73,750	14,225	10,136
73,750	73,800	14,238	10,144
73,800	73,850	14,250	10,151
73,850	73,900	14,263	10,159
73,900	73,950	14,275	10,166
73,950	74,000	14,288	10,174

74,000

At least	But less than	Single	Married filing jointly
74,000	74,050	14,300	10,181
74,050	74,100	14,313	10,189
74,100	74,150	14,325	10,196
74,150	74,200	14,338	10,204
74,200	74,250	14,350	10,211
74,250	74,300	14,363	10,219
74,300	74,350	14,375	10,226
74,350	74,400	14,388	10,234
74,400	74,450	14,400	10,241
74,450	74,500	14,413	10,249
74,500	74,550	14,425	10,256
74,550	74,600	14,438	10,264
74,600	74,650	14,450	10,271
74,650	74,700	14,463	10,279
74,700	74,750	14,475	10,286
74,750	74,800	14,488	10,294
74,800	74,850	14,500	10,301
74,850	74,900	14,513	10,309
74,900	74,950	14,525	10,319
74,950	75,000	14,538	10,331

75,000

At least	But less than	Single	Married filing jointly
75,000	75,050	14,550	10,344
75,050	75,100	14,563	10,356
75,100	75,150	14,575	10,369
75,150	75,200	14,588	10,381
75,200	75,250	14,600	10,394
75,250	75,300	14,613	10,406
75,300	75,350	14,625	10,419
75,350	75,400	14,638	10,431
75,400	75,450	14,650	10,444
75,450	75,500	14,663	10,456
75,500	75,550	14,675	10,469
75,550	75,600	14,688	10,481
75,600	75,650	14,700	10,494
75,650	75,700	14,713	10,506
75,700	75,750	14,725	10,519
75,750	75,800	14,738	10,531
75,800	75,850	14,750	10,544
75,850	75,900	14,763	10,556
75,900	75,950	14,775	10,569
75,950	76,000	14,788	10,581

76,000

At least	But less than	Single	Married filing jointly
76,000	76,050	14,800	10,594
76,050	76,100	14,813	10,606
76,100	76,150	14,825	10,619
76,150	76,200	14,838	10,631
76,200	76,250	14,850	10,644
76,250	76,300	14,863	10,656
76,300	76,350	14,875	10,669
76,350	76,400	14,888	10,681
76,400	76,450	14,900	10,694
76,450	76,500	14,913	10,706
76,500	76,550	14,925	10,719
76,550	76,600	14,938	10,731
76,600	76,650	14,950	10,744
76,650	76,700	14,963	10,756
76,700	76,750	14,975	10,769
76,750	76,800	14,988	10,781
76,800	76,850	15,000	10,794
76,850	76,900	15,013	10,806
76,900	76,950	15,025	10,819
76,950	77,000	15,038	10,831

(Continued)

Instructions for Form 1040EZ

Table header (applies to all sections):

If Form 1040EZ, line 6, is— / **And you are—** / Your tax is—

At least	But less than	Single	Married filing jointly

77,000

At least	But less than	Single	Married filing jointly
77,000	77,050	15,050	10,844
77,050	77,100	15,063	10,856
77,100	77,150	15,075	10,869
77,150	77,200	15,088	10,881
77,200	77,250	15,100	10,894
77,250	77,300	15,113	10,906
77,300	77,350	15,125	10,919
77,350	77,400	15,138	10,931
77,400	77,450	15,150	10,944
77,450	77,500	15,163	10,956
77,500	77,550	15,175	10,969
77,550	77,600	15,188	10,981
77,600	77,650	15,200	10,994
77,650	77,700	15,213	11,006
77,700	77,750	15,225	11,019
77,750	77,800	15,238	11,031
77,800	77,850	15,250	11,044
77,850	77,900	15,263	11,056
77,900	77,950	15,275	11,069
77,950	78,000	15,288	11,081

78,000

At least	But less than	Single	Married filing jointly
78,000	78,050	15,300	11,094
78,050	78,100	15,313	11,106
78,100	78,150	15,325	11,119
78,150	78,200	15,338	11,131
78,200	78,250	15,350	11,144
78,250	78,300	15,363	11,156
78,300	78,350	15,375	11,169
78,350	78,400	15,388	11,181
78,400	78,450	15,400	11,194
78,450	78,500	15,413	11,206
78,500	78,550	15,425	11,219
78,550	78,600	15,438	11,231
78,600	78,650	15,450	11,244
78,650	78,700	15,463	11,256
78,700	78,750	15,475	11,269
78,750	78,800	15,488	11,281
78,800	78,850	15,500	11,294
78,850	78,900	15,513	11,306
78,900	78,950	15,525	11,319
78,950	79,000	15,538	11,331

79,000

At least	But less than	Single	Married filing jointly
79,000	79,050	15,550	11,344
79,050	79,100	15,563	11,356
79,100	79,150	15,575	11,369
79,150	79,200	15,588	11,381
79,200	79,250	15,600	11,394
79,250	79,300	15,613	11,406
79,300	79,350	15,625	11,419
79,350	79,400	15,638	11,431
79,400	79,450	15,650	11,444
79,450	79,500	15,663	11,456
79,500	79,550	15,675	11,469
79,550	79,600	15,688	11,481
79,600	79,650	15,700	11,494
79,650	79,700	15,713	11,506
79,700	79,750	15,725	11,519
79,750	79,800	15,738	11,531
79,800	79,850	15,750	11,544
79,850	79,900	15,763	11,556
79,900	79,950	15,775	11,569
79,950	80,000	15,788	11,581

80,000

At least	But less than	Single	Married filing jointly
80,000	80,050	15,800	11,594
80,050	80,100	15,813	11,606
80,100	80,150	15,825	11,619
80,150	80,200	15,838	11,631
80,200	80,250	15,850	11,644
80,250	80,300	15,863	11,656
80,300	80,350	15,875	11,669
80,350	80,400	15,888	11,681
80,400	80,450	15,900	11,694
80,450	80,500	15,913	11,706
80,500	80,550	15,925	11,719
80,550	80,600	15,938	11,731
80,600	80,650	15,950	11,744
80,650	80,700	15,963	11,756
80,700	80,750	15,975	11,769
80,750	80,800	15,988	11,781
80,800	80,850	16,000	11,794
80,850	80,900	16,013	11,806
80,900	80,950	16,025	11,819
80,950	81,000	16,038	11,831

81,000

At least	But less than	Single	Married filing jointly
81,000	81,050	16,050	11,844
81,050	81,100	16,063	11,856
81,100	81,150	16,075	11,869
81,150	81,200	16,088	11,881
81,200	81,250	16,100	11,894
81,250	81,300	16,113	11,906
81,300	81,350	16,125	11,919
81,350	81,400	16,138	11,931
81,400	81,450	16,150	11,944
81,450	81,500	16,163	11,956
81,500	81,550	16,175	11,969
81,550	81,600	16,188	11,981
81,600	81,650	16,200	11,994
81,650	81,700	16,213	12,006
81,700	81,750	16,225	12,019
81,750	81,800	16,238	12,031
81,800	81,850	16,250	12,044
81,850	81,900	16,263	12,056
81,900	81,950	16,275	12,069
81,950	82,000	16,288	12,081

82,000

At least	But less than	Single	Married filing jointly
82,000	82,050	16,300	12,094
82,050	82,100	16,313	12,106
82,100	82,150	16,325	12,119
82,150	82,200	16,338	12,131
82,200	82,250	16,350	12,144
82,250	82,300	16,363	12,156
82,300	82,350	16,375	12,169
82,350	82,400	16,388	12,181
82,400	82,450	16,400	12,194
82,450	82,500	16,413	12,206
82,500	82,550	16,425	12,219
82,550	82,600	16,438	12,231
82,600	82,650	16,450	12,244
82,650	82,700	16,463	12,256
82,700	82,750	16,475	12,269
82,750	82,800	16,488	12,281
82,800	82,850	16,500	12,294
82,850	82,900	16,513	12,306
82,900	82,950	16,525	12,319
82,950	83,000	16,538	12,331

83,000

At least	But less than	Single	Married filing jointly
83,000	83,050	16,550	12,344
83,050	83,100	16,563	12,356
83,100	83,150	16,575	12,369
83,150	83,200	16,588	12,381
83,200	83,250	16,600	12,394
83,250	83,300	16,613	12,406
83,300	83,350	16,625	12,419
83,350	83,400	16,638	12,431
83,400	83,450	16,650	12,444
83,450	83,500	16,663	12,456
83,500	83,550	16,675	12,469
83,550	83,600	16,688	12,481
83,600	83,650	16,700	12,494
83,650	83,700	16,713	12,506
83,700	83,750	16,725	12,519
83,750	83,800	16,738	12,531
83,800	83,850	16,750	12,544
83,850	83,900	16,763	12,556
83,900	83,950	16,775	12,569
83,950	84,000	16,788	12,581

84,000

At least	But less than	Single	Married filing jointly
84,000	84,050	16,800	12,594
84,050	84,100	16,813	12,606
84,100	84,150	16,825	12,619
84,150	84,200	16,838	12,631
84,200	84,250	16,850	12,644
84,250	84,300	16,863	12,656
84,300	84,350	16,875	12,669
84,350	84,400	16,888	12,681
84,400	84,450	16,900	12,694
84,450	84,500	16,913	12,706
84,500	84,550	16,925	12,719
84,550	84,600	16,938	12,731
84,600	84,650	16,950	12,744
84,650	84,700	16,963	12,756
84,700	84,750	16,975	12,769
84,750	84,800	16,988	12,781
84,800	84,850	17,000	12,794
84,850	84,900	17,013	12,806
84,900	84,950	17,025	12,819
84,950	85,000	17,038	12,831

85,000

At least	But less than	Single	Married filing jointly
85,000	85,050	17,050	12,844
85,050	85,100	17,063	12,856
85,100	85,150	17,075	12,869
85,150	85,200	17,088	12,881
85,200	85,250	17,100	12,894
85,250	85,300	17,113	12,906
85,300	85,350	17,125	12,919
85,350	85,400	17,138	12,931
85,400	85,450	17,150	12,944
85,450	85,500	17,163	12,956
85,500	85,550	17,175	12,969
85,550	85,600	17,188	12,981
85,600	85,650	17,200	12,994
85,650	85,700	17,213	13,006
85,700	85,750	17,225	13,019
85,750	85,800	17,238	13,031
85,800	85,850	17,250	13,044
85,850	85,900	17,263	13,056
85,900	85,950	17,275	13,069
85,950	86,000	17,288	13,081

86,000

At least	But less than	Single	Married filing jointly
86,000	86,050	17,300	13,094
86,050	86,100	17,313	13,106
86,100	86,150	17,325	13,119
86,150	86,200	17,338	13,131
86,200	86,250	17,350	13,144
86,250	86,300	17,363	13,156
86,300	86,350	17,375	13,169
86,350	86,400	17,388	13,181
86,400	86,450	17,400	13,194
86,450	86,500	17,413	13,206
86,500	86,550	17,425	13,219
86,550	86,600	17,438	13,231
86,600	86,650	17,450	13,244
86,650	86,700	17,463	13,256
86,700	86,750	17,475	13,269
86,750	86,800	17,488	13,281
86,800	86,850	17,500	13,294
86,850	86,900	17,513	13,306
86,900	86,950	17,525	13,319
86,950	87,000	17,538	13,331

87,000

At least	But less than	Single	Married filing jointly
87,000	87,050	17,550	13,344
87,050	87,100	17,563	13,356
87,100	87,150	17,575	13,369
87,150	87,200	17,588	13,381
87,200	87,250	17,600	13,394
87,250	87,300	17,613	13,406
87,300	87,350	17,625	13,419
87,350	87,400	17,638	13,431
87,400	87,450	17,650	13,444
87,450	87,500	17,663	13,456
87,500	87,550	17,675	13,469
87,550	87,600	17,688	13,481
87,600	87,650	17,700	13,494
87,650	87,700	17,713	13,506
87,700	87,750	17,725	13,519
87,750	87,800	17,738	13,531
87,800	87,850	17,750	13,544
87,850	87,900	17,763	13,556
87,900	87,950	17,775	13,569
87,950	88,000	17,788	13,581

88,000

At least	But less than	Single	Married filing jointly
88,000	88,050	17,800	13,594
88,050	88,100	17,813	13,606
88,100	88,150	17,825	13,619
88,150	88,200	17,838	13,631
88,200	88,250	17,850	13,644
88,250	88,300	17,863	13,656
88,300	88,350	17,875	13,669
88,350	88,400	17,888	13,681
88,400	88,450	17,900	13,694
88,450	88,500	17,913	13,706
88,500	88,550	17,925	13,719
88,550	88,600	17,938	13,731
88,600	88,650	17,950	13,744
88,650	88,700	17,963	13,756
88,700	88,750	17,975	13,769
88,750	88,800	17,988	13,781
88,800	88,850	18,000	13,794
88,850	88,900	18,013	13,806
88,900	88,950	18,025	13,819
88,950	89,000	18,038	13,831

(Continued)

89,000

If Form 1040EZ, line 6, is–		And you are–	
At least	But less than	Single	Married filing jointly
		Your tax is–	
89,000	89,050	18,050	13,844
89,050	89,100	18,063	13,856
89,100	89,150	18,075	13,869
89,150	89,200	18,088	13,881
89,200	89,250	18,100	13,894
89,250	89,300	18,113	13,906
89,300	89,350	18,125	13,919
89,350	89,400	18,138	13,931
89,400	89,450	18,150	13,944
89,450	89,500	18,163	13,956
89,500	89,550	18,175	13,969
89,550	89,600	18,188	13,981
89,600	89,650	18,200	13,994
89,650	89,700	18,213	14,006
89,700	89,750	18,225	14,019
89,750	89,800	18,238	14,031
89,800	89,850	18,250	14,044
89,850	89,900	18,263	14,056
89,900	89,950	18,275	14,069
89,950	90,000	18,288	14,081

90,000

At least	But less than	Single	Married filing jointly
90,000	90,050	18,300	14,094
90,050	90,100	18,313	14,106
90,100	90,150	18,325	14,119
90,150	90,200	18,338	14,131
90,200	90,250	18,350	14,144
90,250	90,300	18,363	14,156
90,300	90,350	18,375	14,169
90,350	90,400	18,388	14,181
90,400	90,450	18,400	14,194
90,450	90,500	18,413	14,206
90,500	90,550	18,425	14,219
90,550	90,600	18,438	14,231
90,600	90,650	18,450	14,244
90,650	90,700	18,463	14,256
90,700	90,750	18,475	14,269
90,750	90,800	18,488	14,281
90,800	90,850	18,502	14,294
90,850	90,900	18,516	14,306
90,900	90,950	18,530	14,319
90,950	91,000	18,544	14,331

91,000

At least	But less than	Single	Married filing jointly
91,000	91,050	18,558	14,344
91,050	91,100	18,572	14,356
91,100	91,150	18,586	14,369
91,150	91,200	18,600	14,381
91,200	91,250	18,614	14,394
91,250	91,300	18,628	14,406
91,300	91,350	18,642	14,419
91,350	91,400	18,656	14,431
91,400	91,450	18,670	14,444
91,450	91,500	18,684	14,456
91,500	91,550	18,698	14,469
91,550	91,600	18,712	14,481
91,600	91,650	18,726	14,494
91,650	91,700	18,740	14,506
91,700	91,750	18,754	14,519
91,750	91,800	18,768	14,531
91,800	91,850	18,782	14,544
91,850	91,900	18,796	14,556
91,900	91,950	18,810	14,569
91,950	92,000	18,824	14,581

92,000

At least	But less than	Single	Married filing jointly
92,000	92,050	18,838	14,594
92,050	92,100	18,852	14,606
92,100	92,150	18,866	14,619
92,150	92,200	18,880	14,631
92,200	92,250	18,894	14,644
92,250	92,300	18,908	14,656
92,300	92,350	18,922	14,669
92,350	92,400	18,936	14,681
92,400	92,450	18,950	14,694
92,450	92,500	18,964	14,706
92,500	92,550	18,978	14,719
92,550	92,600	18,992	14,731
92,600	92,650	19,006	14,744
92,650	92,700	19,020	14,756
92,700	92,750	19,034	14,769
92,750	92,800	19,048	14,781
92,800	92,850	19,062	14,794
92,850	92,900	19,076	14,806
92,900	92,950	19,090	14,819
92,950	93,000	19,104	14,831

93,000

At least	But less than	Single	Married filing jointly
93,000	93,050	19,118	14,844
93,050	93,100	19,132	14,856
93,100	93,150	19,146	14,869
93,150	93,200	19,160	14,881
93,200	93,250	19,174	14,894
93,250	93,300	19,188	14,906
93,300	93,350	19,202	14,919
93,350	93,400	19,216	14,931
93,400	93,450	19,230	14,944
93,450	93,500	19,244	14,956
93,500	93,550	19,258	14,969
93,550	93,600	19,272	14,981
93,600	93,650	19,286	14,994
93,650	93,700	19,300	15,006
93,700	93,750	19,314	15,019
93,750	93,800	19,328	15,031
93,800	93,850	19,342	15,044
93,850	93,900	19,356	15,056
93,900	93,950	19,370	15,069
93,950	94,000	19,384	15,081

94,000

At least	But less than	Single	Married filing jointly
94,000	94,050	19,398	15,094
94,050	94,100	19,412	15,106
94,100	94,150	19,426	15,119
94,150	94,200	19,440	15,131
94,200	94,250	19,454	15,144
94,250	94,300	19,468	15,156
94,300	94,350	19,482	15,169
94,350	94,400	19,496	15,181
94,400	94,450	19,510	15,194
94,450	94,500	19,524	15,206
94,500	94,550	19,538	15,219
94,550	94,600	19,552	15,231
94,600	94,650	19,566	15,244
94,650	94,700	19,580	15,256
94,700	94,750	19,594	15,269
94,750	94,800	19,608	15,281
94,800	94,850	19,622	15,294
94,850	94,900	19,636	15,306
94,900	94,950	19,650	15,319
94,950	95,000	19,664	15,331

95,000

At least	But less than	Single	Married filing jointly
95,000	95,050	19,678	15,344
95,050	95,100	19,692	15,356
95,100	95,150	19,706	15,369
95,150	95,200	19,720	15,381
95,200	95,250	19,734	15,394
95,250	95,300	19,748	15,406
95,300	95,350	19,762	15,419
95,350	95,400	19,776	15,431
95,400	95,450	19,790	15,444
95,450	95,500	19,804	15,456
95,500	95,550	19,818	15,469
95,550	95,600	19,832	15,481
95,600	95,650	19,846	15,494
95,650	95,700	19,860	15,506
95,700	95,750	19,874	15,519
95,750	95,800	19,888	15,531
95,800	95,850	19,902	15,544
95,850	95,900	19,916	15,556
95,900	95,950	19,930	15,569
95,950	96,000	19,944	15,581

96,000

At least	But less than	Single	Married filing jointly
96,000	96,050	19,958	15,594
96,050	96,100	19,972	15,606
96,100	96,150	19,986	15,619
96,150	96,200	20,000	15,631
96,200	96,250	20,014	15,644
96,250	96,300	20,028	15,656
96,300	96,350	20,042	15,669
96,350	96,400	20,056	15,681
96,400	96,450	20,070	15,694
96,450	96,500	20,084	15,706
96,500	96,550	20,098	15,719
96,550	96,600	20,112	15,731
96,600	96,650	20,126	15,744
96,650	96,700	20,140	15,756
96,700	96,750	20,154	15,769
96,750	96,800	20,168	15,781
96,800	96,850	20,182	15,794
96,850	96,900	20,196	15,806
96,900	96,950	20,210	15,819
96,950	97,000	20,224	15,831

97,000

At least	But less than	Single	Married filing jointly
97,000	97,050	20,238	15,844
97,050	97,100	20,252	15,856
97,100	97,150	20,266	15,869
97,150	97,200	20,280	15,881
97,200	97,250	20,294	15,894
97,250	97,300	20,308	15,906
97,300	97,350	20,322	15,919
97,350	97,400	20,336	15,931
97,400	97,450	20,350	15,944
97,450	97,500	20,364	15,956
97,500	97,550	20,378	15,969
97,550	97,600	20,392	15,981
97,600	97,650	20,406	15,994
97,650	97,700	20,420	16,006
97,700	97,750	20,434	16,019
97,750	97,800	20,448	16,031
97,800	97,850	20,462	16,044
97,850	97,900	20,476	16,056
97,900	97,950	20,490	16,069
97,950	98,000	20,504	16,081

98,000

At least	But less than	Single	Married filing jointly
98,000	98,050	20,518	16,094
98,050	98,100	20,532	16,106
98,100	98,150	20,546	16,119
98,150	98,200	20,560	16,131
98,200	98,250	20,574	16,144
98,250	98,300	20,588	16,156
98,300	98,350	20,602	16,169
98,350	98,400	20,616	16,181
98,400	98,450	20,630	16,194
98,450	98,500	20,644	16,206
98,500	98,550	20,658	16,219
98,550	98,600	20,672	16,231
98,600	98,650	20,686	16,244
98,650	98,700	20,700	16,256
98,700	98,750	20,714	16,269
98,750	98,800	20,728	16,281
98,800	98,850	20,742	16,294
98,850	98,900	20,756	16,306
98,900	98,950	20,770	16,319
98,950	99,000	20,784	16,331

99,000

At least	But less than	Single	Married filing jointly
99,000	99,050	20,798	16,344
99,050	99,100	20,812	16,356
99,100	99,150	20,826	16,369
99,150	99,200	20,840	16,381
99,200	99,250	20,854	16,394
99,250	99,300	20,868	16,406
99,300	99,350	20,882	16,419
99,350	99,400	20,896	16,431
99,400	99,450	20,910	16,444
99,450	99,500	20,924	16,456
99,500	99,550	20,938	16,469
99,550	99,600	20,952	16,481
99,600	99,650	20,966	16,494
99,650	99,700	20,980	16,506
99,700	99,750	20,994	16,519
99,750	99,800	21,008	16,531
99,800	99,850	21,022	16,544
99,850	99,900	21,036	16,556
99,900	99,950	21,050	16,569
99,950	100,000	21,064	16,581

$100,000 or over — use Form 1040

Disclosure, Privacy Act, and Paperwork Reduction Act Notice

The IRS Restructuring and Reform Act of 1998, the Privacy Act of 1974, and the Paperwork Reduction Act of 1980 require that when we ask you for information we must first tell you our legal right to ask for the information, why we are asking for it, and how it will be used. We must also tell you what could happen if we do not receive it and whether your response is voluntary, required to obtain a benefit, or mandatory under the law.

This notice applies to all papers you file with us, including this tax return. It also applies to any questions we need to ask you so we can complete, correct, or process your return; figure your tax; and collect tax, interest, or penalties.

Our legal right to ask for information is Internal Revenue Code sections 6001, 6011, and 6012(a), and their regulations. They say that you must file a return or statement with us for any tax you are liable for. Your response is mandatory under these sections. Code section 6109 requires you to provide your identifying number on the return. This is so we know who you are, and can process your return and other papers. You must fill in all parts of the tax form that apply to you. But you do not have to check the boxes for the Presidential Election Campaign Fund or for the third-party designee. You also do not have to provide your daytime phone number.

You are not required to provide the information requested on a form that is subject to the Paperwork Reduction Act unless the form displays a valid OMB control number. Books or records relating to a form or its instructions must be retained as long as their contents may become material in the administration of any Internal Revenue law.

We ask for tax return information to carry out the tax laws of the United States. We need it to figure and collect the right amount of tax.

If you do not file a return, do not provide the information we ask for, or provide fraudulent information, you may be charged penalties and be subject to criminal prosecution. We may also have to disallow the exemptions, exclusions, credits, deductions, or adjustments shown on the tax return. This could make the tax higher or delay any refund. Interest may also be charged.

Generally, tax returns and return information are confidential, as stated in Code section 6103. However, Code section 6103 allows or requires the Internal Revenue Service to disclose or give the information shown on your tax return to others as described in the Code. For example, we may disclose your tax information to the Department of Justice to enforce the tax laws, both civil and criminal, and to cities, states, the District of Columbia, and U.S. commonwealths and possessions to carry out their tax laws. We may disclose your tax information to the Department of Treasury and contractors for tax administration purposes; and to other persons as necessary to obtain information needed to determine the amount of or to collect the tax you owe. We may disclose your tax information to the Comptroller General of the United States to permit the Comptroller General to review the Internal Revenue Service. We may disclose your tax information to committees of Congress; federal, state, and local child support agencies; and to other federal agencies for the purposes of determining entitlement for benefits or the eligibility for and the repayment of loans. We may also disclose this information to other countries under a tax treaty, to federal and state agencies to enforce federal nontax criminal laws, or to federal law enforcement and intelligence agencies to combat terrorism.

Please keep this notice with your records. It may help you if we ask you for other information. If you have questions about the rules for filing and giving information, please call or visit any Internal Revenue Service office.

We welcome comments on forms. We try to create forms and instructions that can be easily understood. Often this is difficult to do because our tax laws are very complex. For some people with income mostly from wages, filling in the forms is easy. For others who have businesses, pensions, stocks, rental income, or other investments, it is more difficult.

If you have suggestions for making these forms simpler, we would be happy to hear from you. You can send us comments from *www.irs.gov/formspubs*. Click on "More Information" and then on "Give us feedback." Or you can send your comments to Internal Revenue Service, Tax Forms and Publications Division, 1111 Constitution Ave. NW, IR-6526, Washington, DC 20224. Do not send your return to this address. Instead, see the addresses at the end of these instructions.

Although we cannot respond individually to each comment received, we do appreciate your feedback and will consider your comments as we revise our tax forms and instructions.

Estimates of Taxpayer Burden

The table below shows burden estimates based upon current statutory requirements as of December 2015 for taxpayers filing a 2015 1040EZ tax return. Time spent and out-of-pocket costs are presented separately. Time burden is broken out by taxpayer activity, with record keeping representing the largest component. Out-of-pocket costs include any expenses incurred by taxpayers to prepare and submit their tax returns. Examples include tax return preparation and submission fees, postage and photocopying costs, and tax preparation software costs. While these estimates do not include burden associated with post-filing activities, IRS operational data indicate that electronically prepared and filed returns have fewer arithmetic errors, implying lower post-filing burden.

Tax preparation fees and other out-of-pocket costs vary extensively depending on the tax situation of the taxpayer, the type of software or professional preparer used, and the geographic location. Reported time and cost burdens are national averages and do not necessarily reflect a "typical" case. Most taxpayers experience lower than average burden, with taxpayer burden varying considerably by taxpayer type. The average for Form 1040EZ filers is about 5 hours and $40.

If you have comments concerning the time and cost estimates that follow, you can contact us at either one of the addresses shown under *We welcome comments on forms*, earlier.

Estimated Average Taxpayer Burden for Individuals by Activity

Primary Form Filed	Percentage of Returns	Average Time Burden (Hours)					Average Cost (Dollars)
		Total Time	Record Keeping	Tax Planning	Form Completion and Submission	All Other	
1040EZ	12	5	1	1	2	1	$40

Detail may not add to total time due to rounding. Dollars rounded to the nearest $10.

Major Categories of Federal Income and Outlays for Fiscal Year 2014

Income and Outlays. These pie charts show the relative sizes of the major categories of federal income and outlays for fiscal year 2014.

Income

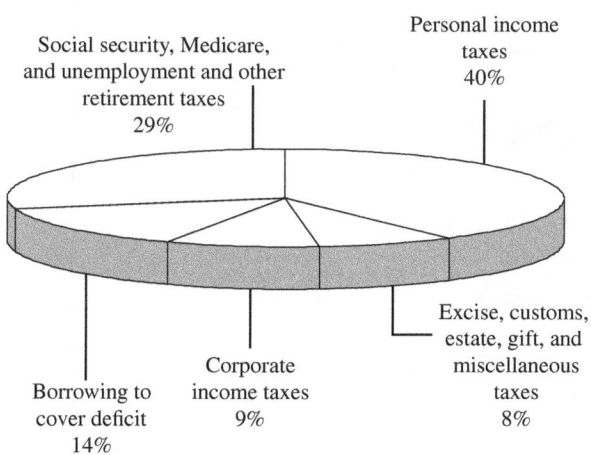

Social security, Medicare, and unemployment and other retirement taxes
29%

Personal income taxes
40%

Borrowing to cover deficit
14%

Corporate income taxes
9%

Excise, customs, estate, gift, and miscellaneous taxes
8%

Outlays*

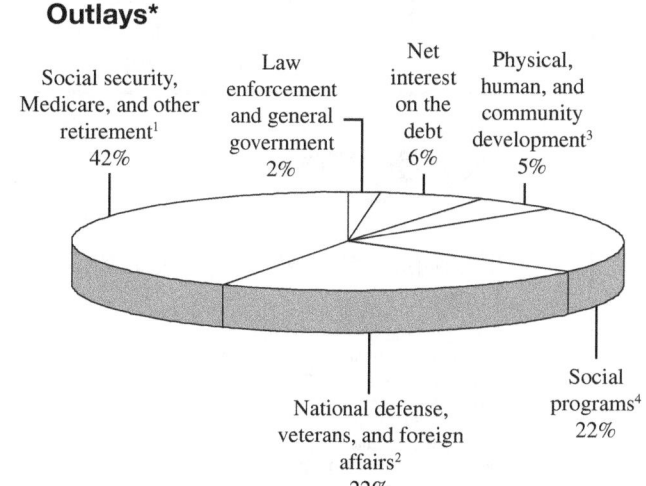

Social security, Medicare, and other retirement[1]
42%

Law enforcement and general government
2%

Net interest on the debt
6%

Physical, human, and community development[3]
5%

National defense, veterans, and foreign affairs[2]
22%

Social programs[4]
22%

* Numbers may not total to 100% due to rounding.

On or before the first Monday in February of each year the President is required by law to submit to the Congress a budget proposal for the fiscal year that begins the following October. The budget plan sets forth the President's proposed receipts, spending, and the surplus or deficit for the Federal Government. The plan includes recommendations for new legislation as well as recommendations to change, eliminate, and add programs. After receipt of the President's proposal, the Congress reviews the proposal and makes changes. It first passes a budget resolution setting its own targets for receipts, outlays, and surplus or deficit. Next, individual spending and revenue bills that are consistent with the goals of the budget resolution are enacted.

In fiscal year 2014 (which began on October 1, 2013, and ended on September 30, 2014), Federal income was $3.021 trillion and outlays were $3.506 trillion, leaving a deficit of $485 billion.

Footnotes for Certain Federal Outlays

1. **Social security, Medicare, and other retirement:** These programs provide income support for the retired and disabled and medical care for the elderly.

2. **National defense, veterans, and foreign affairs:** About 17% of Federal outlays were to equip, modernize, and pay our armed forces and to fund national defense activities; 4% were for veterans' benefits and services; and about 1% were for international activities, including military and economic assistance to foreign countries and the maintenance of United States embassies abroad.

3. **Physical, human, and community development:** These outlays were for agriculture; natural resources; environment; transportation; aid for elementary and secondary education and direct assistance to college students; job training; deposit insurance, commerce and housing credit, and community development; and space, energy, and general science programs.

4. **Social programs:** About 16% of total outlays were for Medicaid, food stamps, temporary assistance for needy families, supplemental security income, and related programs; and the remaining outlays were for health research and public health programs, unemployment compensation, assisted housing, and social services.

Note. The percentage calculations in this section and the dollar chart for outlays exclude undistributed offsetting receipts, which were $88 billion in 2014. In the budget, these receipts are offset against spending in the calculation of the outlay total. These receipts are for the U.S. Government's share of its employee retirement programs, rents and royalties on the Outer Continental Shelf, and proceeds from the sale of assets.

Instructions for Form 1040EZ

Options for *e-filing* your returns—safely, quickly, and easily.

Why do 85% of Americans file their taxes electronically?

- *Security*—The IRS uses the latest encryption technology to safeguard your information.
- *Flexible Payments*—File early; pay by the due date of your return (not counting extensions)—April 18, 2016, for most people.
- *Greater Accuracy*—Fewer errors mean faster processing.
- *Quick Receipt*—Get an acknowledgment that your return was received and accepted.
- *Go Green*—Reduce the amount of paper used.
- *It's Free*—through Free File.
- *Faster Refunds*—Join the eight in 10 taxpayers who get their refunds faster by using direct deposit and *e-file*.

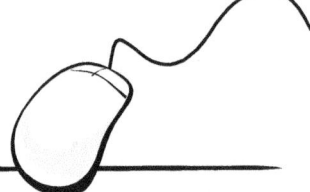

IRS *e-file:* It's Safe. It's Easy. It's Time.

Joining the more than 125 million Americans who already are using *e-file* is easy. Just ask your paid or volunteer tax preparer, use commercial software, or use Free File. IRS *e-file* is the safest, most secure way to transmit your tax return to the IRS. Since 1990, the IRS has processed more than 1 billion *e-filed* tax returns safely and securely. There's no paper return to be lost or stolen.

Most tax return preparers are now required to use IRS *e-file*. If you are asked if you want to *e-file*, just give it a try. IRS *e-file* is now the norm, not the exception. Most states also use electronic filing.

Free Tax Help Available Nationwide

Volunteers are available in communities nationwide providing free tax assistance to low to moderate income (generally under $54,000 in adjusted gross income) and elderly taxpayers (age 60 and older). At selected sites, taxpayers can input and electronically file their own tax return with the assistance of an IRS-certified volunteer.

See *How To Get Tax Help* near the end of these instructions for additional information or visit IRS.gov (Keyword: VITA) for a VITA/TCE site near you!

Do Your Taxes for Free

If your adjusted gross income was $62,000 or less in 2015, you can use free tax software to prepare and *e-file* your tax return. Earned more? Use Free File Fillable Forms.

Free File. This public-private partnership, between the IRS and tax software providers, makes approximately 15 brand name commercial software products and *e-file* available for free. Seventy percent of the nation's taxpayers are eligible.

Just visit *www.irs.gov/freefile* for details. Free File combines all the benefits of *e-file* and easy-to-use software at no cost. Guided questions will help ensure you get all the tax credits and deductions you are due. It's fast, safe, and free.

You can review each software provider's criteria for free usage or use an online tool to find which free software products match your situation. Some software providers offer state tax return preparation for free.

Free File Fillable Forms. The IRS offers electronic versions of IRS paper forms that also can be *e-filed* for free. Free File Fillable Forms is best for people experienced in preparing their own tax returns. There are no income limitations. Free File Fillable Forms does basic math calculations. It supports only federal tax forms.

IRS.gov is the gateway to all electronic services offered by the IRS, as well as the spot to download forms at *www.irs.gov/formspubs*.

Make your tax payments electronically—it's easy.

You can make electronic payments online, by phone, or from a mobile device. Paying electronically is safe and secure. The IRS uses the latest encryption technology and does not store the bank account number you use to submit your payment. When you use any of the IRS electronic payment options, it puts you in control of paying your tax bill and gives you peace of mind. You determine the payment date, and you will receive an immediate confirmation from the IRS. It's easy, secure, and much quicker than mailing in a check or money order. Go to *www.irs.gov/payments* to see all your electronic payment options.

Index to Instructions

Where Do You File?

 Mail your return to the address shown below that applies to you. If you want to use a private delivery service, see *Private delivery services* in Section 4, earlier. Envelopes without enough postage will be returned to you by the post office. Also, include your complete return address.

IF you live in...	THEN use this address if you:	
	Are requesting a refund or are not enclosing a check or money order...	Are enclosing a check or money order...
Florida, Louisiana, Mississippi, Texas	Department of the Treasury Internal Revenue Service Austin, TX 73301-0014	Internal Revenue Service P.O. Box 1214 Charlotte, NC 28201-1214
Alaska, Arizona, California, Colorado, Hawaii, Idaho, Nevada, New Mexico, Oregon, Utah, Washington, Wyoming	Department of the Treasury Internal Revenue Service Fresno, CA 93888-0014	Internal Revenue Service P.O. Box 7704 San Francisco, CA 94120-7704
Arkansas, Illinois, Indiana, Iowa, Kansas, Michigan, Minnesota, Montana, Nebraska, North Dakota, Ohio, Oklahoma, South Dakota, Wisconsin	Department of the Treasury Internal Revenue Service Fresno, CA 93888-0014	Internal Revenue Service P.O. Box 802501 Cincinnati, OH 45280-2501
Alabama, Georgia, Kentucky, New Jersey, North Carolina, South Carolina, Tennessee, Virginia	Department of the Treasury Internal Revenue Service Kansas City, MO 64999-0014	Internal Revenue Service P.O. Box 931000 Louisville, KY 40293-1000
Connecticut, Delaware, District of Columbia, Maine, Maryland, Massachusetts, Missouri, New Hampshire, New York, Pennsylvania, Rhode Island, Vermont, West Virginia	Department of the Treasury Internal Revenue Service Kansas City, MO 64999-0014	Internal Revenue Service P.O. Box 37008 Hartford, CT 06176-7008
A foreign country, U.S. possession or territory*, or use an APO or FPO address, or file Form 2555, 2555-EZ, or 4563, or are a dual-status alien.	Department of the Treasury Internal Revenue Service Austin, TX 73301-0215	Internal Revenue Service P.O. Box 1303 Charlotte, NC 28201-1303

* If you live in American Samoa, Puerto Rico, Guam, the U.S. Virgin Islands, or the Northern Mariana Islands, see Pub. 570.